Praise for
Tracy Rohrer Irons and *Your Untethered Voice*

"*Your Untethered Voice* by Tracy Rohrer Irons is a powerful narrative that chronicles the author's path to self-discovery and healing. This book is not just a personal account; it serves as a beacon of hope, offering readers practical tools and insights to embark on their own journeys toward self-reclamation and inner peace. Irons's candid sharing of her experiences invites readers to find solace, inspiration, and the courage to face their own challenges with resilience and hope."

— Dr. Pam George, Author of *Sparkle: Your Seven-Step Guide to a Joy-Infused Life*

"I found *Your Untethered Voice* so inspirational both for those who feel they have had to deal with disabilities and for those who seek to know themselves. I found myself living Tracy's journey as she endured her time hospitalized to becoming her authentic autonomous self. This book is meant for everyone, with each person taking from it what they need. Tracy touches your soul with her positivity and courage. I was privileged to be one of many lucky teachers who had the joy of instilling in Tracy a love of literature and writing."

— Mary Ann Krzyzanowski, Retired Middle School Language Arts and Social Studies Teacher, Wakarusa, Indiana

"Tracy's story of overcoming a disability and an eating disorder will inspire anyone who might be thinking of giving up on their dreams and goals. Tracy suffered injuries from a car accident at age five, before life had even really begun for her. She learned how to reuse her body while other kids were busy playing. She adapted to her disability before the world was ready to help the disabled on a greater scale, and she learned how to search inside herself for the courage to overcome her darkest demons and untether her voice—the result is *Your Untethered Voice,* in which not only her voice but hope are completely untethered."

— Tyler R. Tichelaar, PhD and Award-Winning Author
of *Narrow Lives* and *The Best Place*

"Through faith and self-discovery, Tracy Rohrer Irons shares her personal journey of suffering a tragedy at a young age that left her feeling hopeless and confused. Her inspirational book, *Your Untethered Voice,* unveils lessons she learned and the value she found in using her voice to share her hopes, dreams, and needs. I highly recommend this book because her true story will empower you with wisdom so you can discover your God-given gifts and experience greater joy, health, and freedom."

— Shelley Lynn, Certified Breakthrough Coach
and Author of *Living Fearlessly Free: A Journey of
Forgiveness, Strength, and Freedom*

"Tracy began her life as an active, vibrant young girl in a beautiful, supportive family. She gently brings you into her life, then gifts you with sweet drops of Wisdom, Kindness, and Love. Her story reads the same as she lives her life. The fast canter of the horses on the cover represents the freedom you will discover as Tracy takes you on a slow walk alongside what otherwise would be treacherous cliffs to navigate. On one side, a life-altering accident, on the other, a battle about control of the body and mind. Trust your guide and enjoy the pace. When you reach the open fields, you will be grateful you embraced your Untethered Voice."

— Cynthia McQuade, Founder of More God Movement
and Proprietor of Renew C&D

"Not only is Tracy Rohrer Irons a living testament of power and resilience, but her book *Your Untethered Voice* exemplifies these qualities and more. It's a must-read for everyone because it illuminates the universal struggle against adversity and the journey toward living independently and authentically. Tracy isn't just a great writer; she's an extraordinary human being. I highly recommend this empowering book for anyone seeking solace or guidance on their journey toward healing and self-discovery. It's among my top three books on personal development and self-healing."

— Zana Kenjar, Founder and CEO of ZK Leadership Learning and International Best-Selling Author of *Becoming A Legacy Leader: A 10-Step Manager's Guide to Unlocking Limitless Opportunities*

"*Your Untethered Voice* is a powerfully written memoir and a must read for anyone facing adversity or challenges to experience a journey of resilience, discovery, and renewal. From the very beginning of her story, Tracy captured my heart with her determination and victorious mindset. Tracy sets a beautiful example of taking the broken pieces and pain in her life and exchanging them for healing, acceptance, and transformation. Through her testimony and collection of beautiful poetry, this book will bring awe, wonder, and thankfulness for the miracle of life and how God truly does work all things together for good."

— Quay Ball, Best-Selling Author of *Your Beautiful Exchange*, Writing Coach for Unleash Your Rising

"Tracy Rohrer Irons provides a masterful and simple path to release the habits and negative mindsets that get in the way of happiness and success. *Your Untethered Voice* is a deeply authentic story of Tracy's personal journey to shift focus from external circumstances to internal strength.

This book is a must-read for anyone seeking support and encouragement on the path of reclaiming their best life."

— Donna Herbel, Founder of Blue Phoenix Learning

"Tracy has opened her heart to give us a glimpse of her amazing determination. Having been a lifelong family friend and being familiar with Tracy's story, I find her very personal account of her life nothing short of compelling."

—Melissa Troxel, Retired Journalist,
Healthcare Worker, and Family Friend

YOUR
UNTETHERED
Voice

Resilience, Discovery, and Renewal Unveiled

Tracy Rohrer Irons

Your Untethered Voice:
Resilience, Discovery, and Renewal Unveiled

Our Voices Creations LLC
Goshen, IN
(574) 202-1921
OurVoicesCreations.com

For information, address:
Tracy Rohrer Irons
TracyRohrerIrons.com
tracyrohrerirons@hotmail.com
tracer7119@msn.com

ISBN: 979-8-9908700-0-0
Library of Congress Control Number: 2024913194

Every attempt has been made to source all quotes properly.
For additional copies or bulk purchases, visit:
TracyRohrerIrons.com
or email: tracyrohrerirons@hotmail.com

Editing: Superior Book Productions
Front Cover Design: Fusion Creative Works
Layout: Superior Book Productions
Book Publishing Coach: Christine Gail
Author Photo: Chris Knight Photography
Author Photo Location: The Garage Coffee Shop, Wakarusa, IN

Dedication

I dedicate this book to the memory of my cousin Ben Rohrer, whose wisdom and generosity in time, talent, and spirit left an indelible mark on this world. Husband, father, son, brother, cousin, and friend, Ben still walks upon this earth in our hearts.

I also dedicate this book to everyone who has ever touched my life because you have made me who I am.

And lastly, I dedicate this book to you, my reader. Together, we will bless the world.

Acknowledgments

Thank you to my parents, Jeff and Clara Rohrer, and my sisters, Deb Filley and Barb Newland, for their trips down memory lane to recall childhood years. Thank you to my treasured childhood and lifelong friend Jennifer Rebecca for her visit in recalling memories from school. You are an inspiration. Thank you for being the kind of friend I can always pick up with like we were never apart even if we have not seen each other for several years. Thank you to Erika Moore, the reference clerk at the Elkhart Public Library, who performed the hard work of searching through the newspaper archives to find the articles relating to my accident and fundraisers. Your time-saving efforts were so appreciated.

Thank you to Stan Cook, who was on the ambulance crew and saved my life the day of my accident in 1976. Thank you to every other nameless ambulance crew and hospital staff member who was involved in saving my life that day. I am eternally grateful.

Thank you to my community of author friends introduced through Unleash Your Rising. I discovered every author needs a group of author friends who encourage and support one another. You have all been so valuable in my book writing journey.

Thank you to Christine Gail, Book Publishing Coach and founder of Unleash Your Rising, for her support in writing this book. Thank you to Shiloh Schroeder of Fusion Creative Works for her work on the front cover design. And many thanks to Tyler R. Tichelaar, Senior Editor, and Larry Alexander, Layout & Design, of Superior Book Productions for their work in bringing this book together.

Contents

Introduction

THIS BOOK CONTAINS THE LESSONS I learned on my journey back to me. The journey took place on the road to healing an eating disorder. I also uncovered tangles in my relationship with disability while, simultaneously, journeying deeper, all the way to my core. These pages contain tools to take readers on a journey back to themselves. I am sharing the insights and lessons I've gained through my journey with the wish that part or all of my knowledge and experience will bring healing, hope, peace, and inspiration to many.

The tools in this book are not for just those who have eating disorders. These tools will put the power back into the hands of anyone who has traded peace for anxiety and joy for grief. Too often we stray away from ourselves as a result of life's wounds, rejections, and emotional hardships. We may pile on shovelfuls of the dirt of perfectionism, obsessive-compulsive disorder, and other dysfunctional behaviors in our attempts to bury those wounds. In the process, we become buried alive and parts of us lose their way amid the darkness of that grave.

We do not have to stay buried. We can become equipped to heal and navigate into our futures in emotional health, peace, and joy. Your maintenance of good emotional health, peace, and joy will be a continuous process because life is continual, and the joys, challenges, and hard things of life happen to all of us for our entire lifespan. But we have not been left destitute in this life; we have been given tools, knowledge, and wisdom that can keep us anchored to our souls where we access our gifts, our talents, our joys, and our very being. May *Your Untethered Voice* be one of the many arrows that point you in a positive direction.

This book, like all books, will speak beyond its pages because books speak into the hearts and minds of their readers. In books, we find stories of insight, thoughts, and ideas we agree with, sometimes things we disagree with, sometimes things that make us say *Wow*, and sometimes things that we decide we'll have to ponder with further thought. Whatever you find in these pages, I hope you will pull up a chair and enjoy reading *Your Untethered Voice: Resilience, Discovery, and Renewal Unveiled.*

Let me spend a moment explaining why I chose the title and the image on the book cover. I grew up in an Amish community. The Amish use horses and buggies for transportation. It was common to see horses and buggies traveling on the road. At stores and other public places, we would see horses tied or tethered to a hitching post while their owners ran errands and conducted business. Back home, the horses usually had a pasture where they could roam and run free. It was a happy sight to see the horses when they were running in their pasture. I could imagine their feeling of joy and freedom. Sometimes, the horses even got loose from their pasture and could be found running down the road or strolling through our backyard (true story). The freedom they found running freely is the freedom I am capturing in *Your Untethered Voice*. It reflects that untethered, no-longer-bound freedom. The setting free of you and the resulting freeing of your voice is what we are celebrating in this book.

Your Untethered Voice starts with my story, and the account of how a sudden shift in my early years occurred. Several years later, I coped with some of my challenges by developing an eating disorder. Disordered eating followed me for many years, and as I continue to give my account of it throughout the book, I weave in the tools of knowledge and healing that helped me and continue to bring growth into my life. Many of the chapters conclude with questions for discussion and reflection because taking time to reflect and meditate upon thoughts often deepens their roots of revelation and facilitates growth. My hope is for you to come away inspired and reaching within yourself to access the deepest parts of you. I've also included several poems I have written.

This book is intended to share my story and the tools that have helped me. Every person's journey of healing is individualized, and this book is not a substitute for professional guidance or therapy. Please consult qualified providers and therapists for guidance. Your judgment is key in applying the thoughts and tools within this book. By proceeding, you agree to these terms. My wish for you is to walk into your future in joy, health, and freedom, taking hold of the opportunity to express the gifts, talents, and strengths you bring to the world.

I've wanted to be a writer ever since I was a child. I used to write stories of finding an abandoned mansion to live in and explore. The mansion was always complete with hidden doors and secret passageways. I did not keep any of the stories I wrote. They are long gone, but my passion never died. It did get buried for many years when I thought it was never going to come into being. But my sleeping dream finally awoke.

I didn't know until I started writing this book how widely popular the subject of voice is. My book title came from a divinely inspired message I received, which you will read about. However, the message of voice is an important message being sent to many and is a valuable summons for every human. We are all here by divine design to share the special gifts inside each of us. We share ourselves through voice: our hopes, our dreams, our needs. I am so glad you are here with me. Together, let's explore the message of *Your Untethered Voice.*

I am amazed when I consider all the billions and trillions of people who have ever lived, each with a story all their own. Not everyone has untethered their voice, though, to share that story. I hope by sharing mine, you'll be inspired to share yours. Let me begin by telling you what my life was like before the incident that caused me to tether mine.

When I was three, I remember going to the property where we were building our house in the country. I would go there with my dad and Grandpa Rohrer; sometimes only I went with them because my sisters were in school, and sometimes all three of us girls went. I remember climbing in and out of the hole that Dad and Grandpa were digging for construction preparations. The scene was a child's playground.

In December of that year, we moved into our brand-new house. My sisters, who are twins, shared a bedroom, and I had my own room. We soon got to know our new neighbors and their children near our ages. Lots of playtime with the neighbors, when not attending to other cares and family activities, became the name of the game.

My mom recalls it was not uncommon to find me playing by myself in my room after having played for a time outside with my sisters and my neighbors. I imagine she often found me listening to size 45 records on my record player, rocking to the tunes of "Happy Birthday, Sweet Sixteen," "Hooray for Hazel," or "The Little Drummer Boy." I've discovered, coincidentally, when God created me, he created me on the introverted side, thriving best with lots of time to myself. My mom also often found me by myself swinging on the homemade rope swing attached to one of the big trees in our backyard. Singing and swinging—that is what I liked to do out there.

We continued to grow and flourish in our new home. My sisters and I often took walks in our woods, climbed trees, and built forts. We had the unfortunate experience, more than once, of contracting poison ivy, but such were the joys of country life. We also enjoyed campouts with the neighborhood children at their homes, as well as family campfires. Winter consisted of making snow angels as we played outside until we got too cold.

I learned how to ride a bike. I learned how to tie my shoes. And I finally caught on to baseball. As kindergarten neared, I looked forward to riding the school bus with my sisters, who were now going into third grade. I also looked forward to meeting new friends and playing on the school playground. I don't specifically remember my first day of school, nor the few days after that of my half-day morning kindergarten.

But I do remember the day my mom and I went to Kmart after my morning kindergarten to pick up the new winter coats from layaway my sisters and I were getting. My sisters' coats were blue, my favorite color, and they were furry and fluffy. My coat was tan. While my sisters were still in school that day, Mom and I had also gone to Burger Chef for lunch, the place of the best burgers, in my five-year-old opinion. I sat across the table from Mom, happily eating my burger. That is what I remember from September 28, 1976.

That day is when this story begins. I hope you will continue the journey with me. Welcome to the vista of my book! We will begin with a bit of poetry before this first chapter, then travel on from there. Each chapter will also conclude with poetry I've written. Relax, take a deep breath in, and slowly let it out. I hope you enjoy your journey!

Tracy Rohrer Irons

Just Breathe...

Poem

Welcome, Morning Sunshine

Welcome, morning sunshine,
Welcome into my heart.
We have new thoughts to discover
New wisdom to impart.

With your radiance of hope and wonder,
Inspire human hearts.
Give to them your essence.
Readers, get ready, start.

Now listen with your spirit
And that mighty rushing wind,
That still, small voice within you
That speaks and calls again.

We walk beside still waters,
We lie in pastures green,
We climb the tallest mountains,
And view the wonders seen.

The vista lies within us,
Its beauties we behold.
We wrap our arms around it,
Its treasures make us bold.

We grow into believing
Vista's gifts were made by God.
We have full access to
This clay, this wondrous sod.

Chapter 1
Fashioning a Newness of Life

*"Life is deep; you've got to go deep to
experience and grasp it."*
— Tracy Rohrer Irons

SEPTEMBER 28, 1976, WAS A normal day like any other
at my country home surrounded by wooded areas
and cornfields. I was returning to my house with
my neighbor in the bright afternoon sunshine after a
brief visit to her house. We were walking along the side
of the road. As we neared my house, I caught sight of my
shoelace untied on my sneaker. I bent down to tie my
shoe. The car had just crossed over the hill, and the driv-
er did not see me because of the blinding sun. Suddenly,
my world went dark, and so did my memory of the next
few weeks.

The impact sent me flying into the air. I landed along
the side of the road. Unconscious but alive. And I lost my
shoe. If measured by the world's standards, I lost much
more when I suffered a traumatic brain injury that day.

Mom called Dad at work. Dad was inside the shop at
the time instead of out on the machinery, so he could take

the call right away. He met us at the hospital. My grandpa worked with the same employer as my dad so he learned what had happened. He met my parents at the hospital soon after he got off work.

At the hospital, I remained unconscious with labored breathing. X-rays and scans did not show the injuries. "Prepare for the worst," the doctor told my parents. My parents held on to hope and prayed. After three days, I was transferred to Rush-Presbyterian-St. Luke's Medical Center, a trauma hospital in Chicago, an hour and a half away. When I arrived with labored breathing, the staff knew immediately what to look for and identified the cause as a puncture in the lining of my left lung due to a broken rib. A tube was placed to drain the blood and fluid collecting around my lung. A tracheostomy was performed to further assist my breathing.

Additional x-rays brought to light that my left arm and pinky finger were broken, and my left hip was dislocated with the ball of the femur misplaced from the socket. My eyes remained open at first, so the medical staff had to tape them shut to prevent them from drying out. A syringe-fed feeding tube was placed in my abdomen since I could not eat while in a coma.

My mom was able to stay in Chicago through a housing program the hospital had in place for patients and their families. The hospital was a teaching hospital, so she stayed in a dormitory room with a bed, drawers, a small closet, and a sink. The bathrooms were down the hall. A well-lit underground tunnel connected the dormitory and the hospital, which provided safety for traversing back and forth. Mom frequently brought a tape player to her three daily visits with me. She played a cassette tape containing music, as well as messages from my two older sisters.

A few weeks into my stay, my abdomen began to swell. The doctors did not know what was causing the swelling, so they performed exploratory surgery and discovered my gallbladder and a portion of my small intestine were infected. The surgeons removed both. My gallbladder burst immediately after they abstracted it, and the doctors determined the infection had entered through the feeding tube.

As I lay in my hospital bed in a semi-coma for eight weeks, I grew two inches. "She must have been very healthy before the accident," the medical staff commented. My mom replied, "It must have been all the lotion she ate." As a child, I liked to eat Jergen's lotion, though my mom didn't approve and kept trying to stop me. The reality was I grew two inches because of the high doses of nutrients the hospital staff was feeding me.

Scientists say coma patients can still hear things spoken to them while comatose. I remember hearing and seeing my sisters when they visited; they reported the neighbors had gotten a new dog. For some other memories, I'm not certain whether I was in a semi-coma or awake.

One stuffed monkey, which came to the hospital amid the many cards, flowers, and gifts sent by well-wishers, took on a special assignment. Whenever Dr. Joe visited me, he picked up the monkey and twirled its tail. One day, I smiled as he did so, the first sign I was coming out of the semi-coma. I still have the monkey.

I'm pretty certain some of my memories took place after I woke. I remember a nurse reading to me in the middle of the night when I was still in the ICU. I also remember the staff letting me hold a baby, a fellow ICU patient, which was a delight to my five-year-old girl self. Holding that baby was good therapy for both that infant and me, I'm sure.

I remember the oxygen tent they sometimes put me in. At first, it brought mixed feelings of fear and isolation, but then it became a bit of a fun adventure, like a building-a-fort kind of adventure. My imagination was likely encouraged by my mom and the nurses. The tent was also a relief because, before the tent, I had to wear an oxygen mask. Once I woke from the coma, the oxygen mask was no longer an option because I was terrified and felt claustrophobic every time it was put on. Thankfully, there were other options, such as the tent.

My memories of the hospital after I woke seem to span a couple of months, though they actually only spanned three weeks. A few days after waking, the feeding tube was removed, and I was moved out of the ICU and into a semi-private room. My grandma, aunt, and cousin, who is a year and a half younger than me, came to visit. My cousin and I sat on my bed (I was propped up with pillows) and ate popsicles.

Getting me back on solid foods was a priority. I had to be on solid foods with no feeding tube before I could be released to go to the rehabilitation center. With my gallbladder removed and colon resectioned, food didn't stay down well. The medical staff discovered they had removed the feeding tube too soon, so they had to make an incision and reinsert it for a short while. I was again put on a liquid diet, and solid foods were slowly introduced until, finally, the feeding tube was removed for good.

I remember going to the operating room only once in the hospital, even though I had been there more than once during my coma. As my family and I look back, we are unsure if the surgery I recall was to reinsert the feeding tube or an exploratory procedure to check on a possible infection of my tracheostomy site. In this, my first surgery of recollection, I learned about the food and drink abstention and the dreaded ether used in those days. I remember lying in bed waiting to go into the OR after being prepped for surgery. I was distraught with thirst and did not understand, at that age, the need for no drink. The nurse did her best to console me and, in her mercy, gave me a few ice chips.

I grew to detest the anesthesia mask and the ether itself. The distress from the mask on my face and the smell and taste of the ether were awful. As I drifted off to sleep, the drifting was accompanied by dizziness and a slowly fading sense of sight and sound. Waking was accompanied by nausea and vomiting. Later, when I was in first grade, I had one more surgery with the ether mask. I was relieved in subsequent surgeries when the medical community switched to IV sedation.

As my body continued to heal during my days in the semi-private room, I was so weak I could not lift my head. More than once, when I was in the room with no caregiver or visitor, as I lay in bed, my head slid off the pillow and lodged between the mattress and guardrail. Because I could not lift my head, I had to wait for someone to come. That was a frightening experience. Eventually, someone would come in and place my head back on the pillow.

I left the hospital a few days before Christmas and went straight to the Rehabilitation Institute of Chicago (RIC), which is now the Shirley Ryan Ability Lab. I sat in the backseat of the car and someone held me since I could not support myself. The rehabilitation was structured for the patients to engage in therapies Monday through Friday, with the option to go home on weekends. Christmas was conveniently on a Saturday that year so I was able to be home for Christmas!

Rehabilitation consisted of lots of therapies, especially physical therapy. My therapies included pool therapy some days. I was not a fan of pool therapy because I did not like to change my clothes extra times each day.

Though, the ability to dress oneself is part of rehabilitation, so there were hidden benefits. Getting dressed is actually a function of occupational therapy, which focuses on performing the skills needed in daily life. For children, many occupational therapy sessions are more like play, with things like activity boards containing buttons, snaps, and zippers. Plus, there are crafts and puzzles.

In speech therapy, we worked on increasing my voice volume. Speech therapy also works on the mechanics of eating. Early in recovery, I had difficulty eating a peanut butter sandwich; the peanut butter stuck to the roof of my mouth, and I struggled to get it dislodged. One speech therapy activity that sticks out in my mind is working on the "L" sound. I just realized that particular exercise was instrumental in speaking as well as eating and likely helped me get the peanut butter off the roof of my mouth.

Recreational therapy was held in the evenings when the patients gathered in the game room to play air hockey, board games, and other activities. I participated in a reserved manner. I did not enjoy recreational therapy fully. Sometimes, I would have rather been left alone and had time to myself. One reason may have been because I am introverted. We introverts simply enjoy being by ourselves. Another possible reason I did not enjoy recreational therapy was because I was homesick.

I progressed and was released from rehab in March 1977. I still used a wheelchair because I was unable to walk. I returned to kindergarten for the last few weeks of school. The janitor constructed a desk to accommodate my wheelchair. There were no disability accommodation laws in 1977 in Indiana, and many public places had no handicap-adapted restroom stalls, but my school adapted a stall in the restroom. At the end of that school year, my parents and the teacher decided it would be in my best interest to repeat kindergarten the following school year.

A physical therapist visited our home to continue physical therapy. When the school year started, he also visited the school for my therapy. I was uncomfortable and embarrassed by having to leave the classroom and being singled out. I do not remember many details from my second kindergarten year, but I do remember another physically disabled girl attending. She could walk and had braces on her legs. I struggled to identify with her because I struggled to identify with my disability. In my mind, my disability was a half-truth. It stayed on the fringes of re- ality. As much as we try to push truth away, to deny its existence, truth never leaves us. It only gets buried inside. Buried truth leads to confusion—confusion on the surface and confusion below.

The other physically disabled girl did not attend our school after kindergarten, and for the rest of my grade school and high school years, I was one of the very few physically disabled students in my school.

As my second year of kindergarten progressed, I be- came strong enough to use a walker with the aid of a brace to stabilize my pelvis because my hip joint was still dis- placed. I was glad for the walker because the feeling of independence was rewarding. I did not like the feeling of someone pushing my wheelchair without asking me. A wheelchair serves the user as their method of mobility, and it becomes a tool of their will and self-determination. Pushing my wheelchair against my will without asking happened mostly with other children during recess at school, but also at other play times with other children. By all rights, kids have a natural curiosity and want to play, and a wheelchair can be a new object to explore. I believe my teacher put a stop to other students pushing my wheelchair against my will, or the activity fizzled out. I simply used it to fuel my determination to walk. The sit- uation was a personal irritant but never became a threat or bullying. We lived in a community of supportive people. I never felt bullied or teased during my elementary or secondary years of school.

The winter of my first-grade year, I had surgery to release a tight adductor muscle in my left leg and was placed in a hip spica cast—a full-body cast that goes from the belly button to the toes. Sometimes, one of the legs has a cast only to the knee while the other leg is fully-casted. Mine was fully-casted on both legs, and I was in it for six weeks. After the cast came off, I had to wear it at night as a night splint for four more weeks. The surgery helped my left hip go back into place. I no longer wore the brace after surgery, and as I recovered and grew stronger, I was able to walk independently without a walker.

As I relearned to walk after the brain injury, I perceived my balance and dizziness as my new normal state and did not know I had ataxia. In fact, I did not know my experience of a slight swaying feeling was dizziness. Without realizing it, I also assumed medical professionals knew exactly what I was experiencing in my body. Due to their brain development stage, children have limited perception and will take their experiences as truth. I always had difficulty with my balance, but I did not realize until my forties that my balance problem included dizziness. Others did not know because I did not know…and I did not tell them because I did not know I did not know.

Between third and fourth grade, I had a tendon transfer surgery on my left arm to help my left hand open more instead of being tightly clenched all the time. I wanted to be done with surgeries after that. After I came home from the rehabilitation center in 1977, my mom and I continued home therapy. Somewhere around the age of nine or ten, I informed my mom I did not want to do therapy anymore.

I did not recall telling my mom that until my mom recently mentioned it. But I can picture myself saying it because I remember just wanting to be done with therapy so I could just enjoy living life. When I asked if she thought I had lost any ground on improvement after we stopped therapy, she said no and that therapy, at that point, was more about simply trying to maintain range of motion.

My good friend during my early elementary years recalls I was stubborn back then in the sense that I was strong and wanted to do things myself. As she shared that description with me, the word autonomous came to my mind, and I was finally able to describe my drive for independence, which I remember so well. *The Cambridge Dictionary* defines autonomous as "independent and having the power to make your own decisions."

Looking back, I see how much a child with a disability wants to do things "the normal way." All humans have an innate desire to be normal, not to be singled out as different. We want to fit in. Growing up, the desire to be normal accompanied me. I shunned the label of disabled and tried to live as normally as I could. I now know the beauty of being able to assimilate our disabilities, or whatever "differentness" we have, into who we are and to make that "who we are" into our normal.

I'm grateful for the move today to remove the negative stigma of being different. People have discovered that trying to mold everyone into being normal has not worked. Now there is a movement to be inclusive of differences. I hope we continue to redefine normal as seeking to be our real, authentic self and abnormal as seeking to be anything other than the real you. When we accept the real self on the outside and the true self on the inside, we can lead more authentic and fulfilling lives.

On September 28, 5-year-old Tracy Rohrer, daughter of Jeff and Clara Rohrer, was seriously injured when she was hit by a car. She remains in a semi-coma at St. Luke's Hospital in Chicago.

"TRACY ROHRER" BENEFIT GOSPEL SING

featuring

TRACES   KING'S WITNESS   MASTER'S

December 4, 1976 7:30–9:00 P.M.

NORTHWOOD AUDITORIUM

FREE WILL OFFERING

Benefit Planned For Rohrer Girl

A musical benefit for Tracy Rohrer, 5, daughter of Mr. and Mrs. Jeff Rohrer, Goshen Rt. 7, who was struck by a car Sept. 28 while playing, will be at 7:30 p.m. Saturday, in the NorthWood High School auditorium.

The girl is in a semi-coma in St. Lukes Hospital, Chicago. Friends of the family say that the child's bill, thus far, is more than $20,000 and is covered only partially by insurance.

Featured at the benefit will be gospel group singing, with performances by King's Witness Quartet, Elkhart, and the Masters Quartet and Traces, both of Wakarusa. A free will offering will be taken for the child's benefit. Donations may be made in care of Carl Hunsberger, 65775 C.R. 7, Goshen Rt. 5.

The Love That Never Ends

The love that never ends

Of family and friends

Held within its hands

Borne upon its wings

Wrapped up in its arms.

Benefit for Tracy Rohrer

A benefit chicken barbeque will be held in Wakarusa for Tracy Rohrer, Friday, November 19. The benefit will be held at the Wakarusa Public Library from 3:00 to 7:00 p.m.

Tracy, 5, is the daughter of Mr. and Mrs. Jeffrey Rohrer of C.R 7 in Wakarusa. The young girl was hit by a car in front of her home on September 28. She has been in St. Lukes Presbyterian Hospital in Chicago in a semi-coma. In the past three weeks, Tracy has had three operations two of these were classified as major.

Tickets for the carry-out-only barbeque are available at the door or through Cook's Cones and Sundaes in Wakarusa, the U.S. Mail in Wakarusa and the Wakarusa Pharmacy. Julie Nickerson, sister of Tracy's father, has tickets also, at her home in Nappanee—1003 East Centennial. Her phone number is 773-7044.

Any questions about the benefit will be answered by Darrell Schwartz in Wakarusa at 862-4211.

Poem

The Shadow of Time

The shadow of time
The foster of your soul
The creator of imaginations
Turning parts into whole.

The chasm of the abyss,
Looking far beyond,
Searching the unknown,
Fashioning a bond.

Bonding to the future,
Lassoing the past,
Bringing them together,
Heralding things that last.

Reaching deep within you,
Bringing out the gold,
You are not too young now,
And you are not too old.

You can find a video of "The Shadow of Time" on my YouTube channel at:

https://www.youtube.com/watch?v=kczncPD9BN8

I will be posting more poetry videos on YouTube as well.

Chapter 2
Finding the Way Out
of an Eating Disorder

MY FIRST TWO ORTHOPEDIC SURGERIES, in first grade and the summer before fourth grade, were elective surgeries to try to improve function. My next surgery was more out of dire need. I was unprepared for it.

After regaining the ability to walk, my left foot pointed inward due to spasticity. Somewhere in my thirteenth year, the stress of that abnormal gait started causing a deformity in my left foot. Walking became more and more challenging because my foot started to rotate on its side, leaving me walking on the outside of my foot.

I buried my struggles with my foot and withdrew more and more inside myself in despair, not sharing my hardships. I did not realize my struggles at first. I was occupied with being an active person and entering my adolescent years with all of their own emotional challenges. Believing my physical disability was mentally and emotionally conquered and a person could just be "done with it," I hoped never to have to deal with its emotional difficulties. This led me to bury my emotional struggles so deeply that even I could not access or identify them.

During the same months the foot deformity was progressing, I developed the eating disorder anorexia nervosa. Anorexia nervosa is a mental health disease in which a
person restricts eating and purposely loses weight. I was
about five feet tall and weighed eighty-five pounds, dropping to sixty-five pounds at my lowest weight.

Because of the foot deformity, I fell down so much that
I finished the last few weeks of school at home. I had surgery in June of 1985 to reconstruct the bones in my left foot
and to reset the femur to align my leg in a better position.
The doctor planned to put a pin in my hip instead of cutting the femur bone, but I was too thin to allow for a pin
at the hip joint because a cushioning of fat was needed
between the pin and the skin.

The orthopedic doctor then ran blood tests to diag-
nose the anorexia officially. Because of my low weight, my
bones took longer to heal. I completed the first two months
of my eighth-grade year at home, being homeschooled by
two teachers who came to my house. That was before the
days of the Internet and online school.

At fourteen, I worked with a registered dietitian,
gained weight, and got back on the road of eating. I
achieved weights I personally judged as acceptable and
well. My orthopedic doctor, who had done the foot/femur
surgery, recommended a weight of one hundred pounds
based on my five-foot height at that time. I reached that
weight around the age of fifteen or sixteen. Later, even
though I grew taller, I kept that weight as my goal because
I remembered his words. I weighed one hundred or a few
pounds over in high school. I recall it because I only had
to gain five to ten pounds to reach the one-hundred-ten-
pound requirement to participate in my school's annual
blood drive held in the spring. After the blood drive, I
would purposely lose those few pounds.

Once the blood drive in my senior year was over, I continued the weight loss as the plans and preparations for life after graduation ensued. I was now entering adult life with new and exciting responsibilities. I justified the weight loss because I was busy with the plans, so I made "busy with plans" into an excuse. I have since learned that when we are in a healthy place of loving ourselves, we take action steps to give time and attention to our body's needs.

I did not seek mental health counseling for my eating disorder because, at that time, mental health counseling had a negative stigma in society. I also had the mindset "Christians don't get counseling because they should get counsel only from God or, at most, their pastor." So, my unhealthy relationship with food continued.

I fell into a pattern of eating only at night or keeping my food intake restricted if I did eat during the day. This pattern was born out of obsession and compulsion. It was also a way to allow my mind to focus on other things throughout the day and avoid taking the time to eat, which seemed to allow me to achieve more. In a subtle manner, this pattern also functioned as a reward system, rewarding myself for eating little or nothing earlier in the day. I tried to bury the truth of that reward effect, but it was there.

My eating disorder morphed out of restrictive eating into binge eating. It was never binge and purge because I hate throwing up, but binge and not eat, with the goal of keeping my weight below the healthy BMI range. Maintaining my weight below the healthy BMI range gave me a sense of owning my own private place inside myself, a room, if you will, of isolation and safety.

If I did eat excess or fall into binging, I counteracted it by not eating, sometimes for as long as two days. Episodes of binging and then not eating continued to mingle until my mid-twenties when I got tired of feeling so stuffed that I felt sick after binging, sometimes needing to stay in bed the next day until the nausea wore off. I decided staying in bed because of my stupidity and lack of self-control was ridiculous and hindering my life , so I decided I was done with the binging.

In my twenties, my weight hovered around the ninety- to ninety-eight-pound range. Any visits to the doctor often included advice that I needed to gain weight because my weight was too low. These words reassured me I was staying away from weighing too much. In my adult years, my eating pattern became more consistently eating only at night. Again, there were times when I tried to break that pattern and fix myself by eating two to three times a day instead of once, but I'd fall back into the once-a-day eating.

As my relationship with God and my biblical knowledge grew, I became interested in fasting for its spiritual power and the life force breakthroughs it can bring. I fasted numerous times, praying for deliverance from the eating disorder. I was not getting the desired breakthrough results surrounding the eating disorder and asked myself, "What if God wants me to do more, but I'm rejecting his instruction and not hearing his guidance because I am not willing to hear it and do it? What if he wants me to go to counseling or even something else?"

This is an example of what happens to all of us when we refuse to heed that still, small voice within us. We question it, ignore it, or keep ourselves too far away from it to even hear it. Rejecting that voice is exactly what I was doing because I was not yet ready to hear it.

The Key Was My Relationship with Me

I wanted God to take responsibility for healing my eating disorder. I wanted him to do all of the work because

I was not confident the steps I would take could untangle the knotted-up mess inside. I wanted my relationship with God to be the key to unlock the door, but the key to unlock the door was my relationship with me. That's where the key really lay.

I've learned to look deep inside. The eating disorder kept me out of the inside. The pattern of eating mainly at night was an avenue of comfort. I was able to anticipate the food and allow that anticipation to provide a distraction from the pain inside, even though I did not know the true identity of that pain.

Developing an Eating Disorder

Dr. Pallavi Suyog Uttekar defines eating disorders as a range of psychological conditions that cause severe and persistently abnormal eating behaviors. People who suffer from these disorders use their unhealthy eating patterns to cope with distressing thoughts and emotions. While once considered a psychological condition, newer research is indicating other genetic and biological factors can play into an eating disorder, as well. Let's look at some factors that can play into the development of disordered eating. Be aware that there are many factors, and it will vary from person to person which factors, or which combination of them, will play into their eating disorder.

- **Biological factors:** Research indicates genetics can play a role in eating disorders.
- **Psychological factors:** People with eating disorders often have underlying psychological issues, such as low self-esteem, perfectionism, obsessive-compulsive disorder, and difficulty handling emotions.
- **Environmental factors:** Environmental factors may include societal pressure to be thin, a history

of trauma, a family history of eating disorders, and difficult life events, such as the death of a loved one.
- **Cultural factors:** Some cultures place an emphasis on thinness, linking thinness to success, morality, or beauty.

According to Steven Zauderer of Cross River Therapy, in an article dated September 19, 2023, one person dies every fifty-two minutes from an eating disorder. While doing research for this book, I was surprised to learn that eating disorders have a genetic risk factor, as stated above. According to Zauderer, 28-74 percent of people at risk inherit their risk through genetic ties. Genes, chromosomes, neurotransmitters, hormones, and cannabinoid receptors can all affect an eating disorder.

Eating disorders affect people of all races, genders, and age groups. Women with physical disabilities are at higher risk of an eating disorder. The extra challenges of disability compound the risk. People with diet-related chronic conditions, such as diabetes and irritable bowel syndrome, are also at higher risk for eating disorders.

While eating disorders may often be associated with being underweight, only 6 percent of people with disordered eating are underweight, according to eating disorder statistics from ANAD (National Association of Anorexia Nervosa & Associated Disorders). More often, people who are not underweight meet the standards of disordered eating criteria. Unhealthy weight loss measures used by anyone of any size are considered disordered eating. By using unhealthy measures, a person can increase their risk of developing a chronic pattern of disordered eating. Therefore, developing and maintaining a healthy relationship with food, body weight, and body image is very important.

Approximately thirty million Americans have an eating disorder, and seventy million globally. While eating disorders are popularly viewed as affecting females, surprisingly, ten million men in America will have an eating disorder within their lifetime. Only 6 percent of Americans with eating disorders are medically diagnosed, reducing the probability of getting treatment. With proper treatment, 60 percent of eating disorder patients recover fully, but only one in ten people with an eating disorder ever seek treatment. This book will not cover everything there is to know about eating disorders. I encourage you to seek further resources to study the topic.

By my thirties, I had given up trying to fix my eating pattern and do it differently because the pattern had become comfortably my normal, and it worked for me. Trying to fix it was too hard and exhausting because I didn't know how. I liked the ease of being able to get up in the morning and get busy with my day, giving no thought to food or bothering with it until evening. I truly felt I could get more done that way. My body had adjusted to that eating pattern, and I had no hunger pangs throughout the day. Often, I was not even hungry at night, but I ate because I knew I had to eat. When we repeatedly ignore hunger cues, we mentally lose touch with them, and over time, we may even cause our hunger hormones, leptin and ghrelin, to become disrupted or imbalanced. Ghrelin signals we are hungry, and leptin signals our fullness or satiety level.

I also remained comfortable with my pattern of undereating, and I still liked being too thin and below the recommended BMI. When I went to doctor appointments and was told my weight was too low, it made me feel good about myself. My low weight felt like an accomplishment. I reasoned that I felt good, had a good energy level, and had no medical conditions like diabetes, high blood pressure, or organ diseases, so I must be healthy and eating right. I also reasoned that, in light of my disability, I should stay lighter to avoid putting stress on my joints. With all of those reasons in mind, I solidified that my weight must be good right where it was.

Many times throughout the years, I asked myself, "Why do I have this eating disorder? Is it because of social reasons, or is it a way of dealing with my disability?" Although I would ask that question, I never paused long enough to get an answer because I did not believe I could get the answer. I thought it was buried so deep that I could not dig it up, and when I did try to think about it, my thoughts became confusing, jumbled, and chaotic, like bumper cars at a carnival. This situation happened because, truthfully, I did not want to know; knowing was a scary prospect. If I knew, then I might have to deal with it, and if I dealt with it, what other tool would be left to hold me together? Eating disorders are coping mechanisms. They serve the same coping purpose as other addictions.

People may want to know how the struggle started when they embark on healing an eating disorder or any emotional difficulty that stands in their way. Knowing how or why it started is unnecessary to begin your healing, but the revelation of why may come as you travel along the road of healing. The only thing necessary to begin is a determination to heal, which often comes in the form of, *"I've had enough!* This thing is not serving me, and it's ruining my life. I'm done with it, and I want to be free." This is known as the point at which an adaptive skill, tool, or strategy that worked for us no longer works as well and becomes maladaptive. The person realizes it is holding them back and does not align with the life they hope and aspire for.

The point of *enough* came for me later in life. After enjoying many years of walking independently, around age forty, I started having more difficulty with my balance and started using a cane. By age forty-seven or forty-eight, I started using a walker, after putting it off for too long. Nine staples in the back of my head was my wake-up call. In between the period of cane to walker use, I sank into despair, with the dread of early decline that many people with a disability face. When decline occurs in the midst of perfectionism, low self-worth, and low self-confidence, it also includes a lot of self-doubt and self-blame, which all lead to confusion.

At that point, my obsessive food thoughts and reasonings were racing around in my mind so much that it was hard to think clearly about anything. One day, I stood in my kitchen and looked out the patio door at the sunshine, longing simply to enjoy the day without these cares and thoughts of food overtaking my mind.

So, I took a step closer to beginning my journey. I did not know which eating disorder I had. I had been to a therapist for a couple of sessions in my thirties and told her I wanted help with anorexia. She looked at my stature and told me I did not have anorexia, which left me confused. The only eating disorders I knew of at that time were the ones most frequently talked about: anorexia nervosa and bulimia. I did not know there were others. The therapist would have best served me by asking me why I believed I had an eating disorder and helping me explore the thought. That is why it is vital to work with a therapist who specializes in eating disorders. Eating disorders are complex, so they require someone trained in them to counsel those with them.

Some of the other eating disorders include:

- Binge eating disorder
- ARFID: avoidant/restrictive food intake disorder

- OSFED: other specified feeding or eating disorder
- UFED: unspecified feeding or eating disorder

By sharing the names, I simply want to bring awareness to disordered eating and that there can be numerous forms. Your medical or mental health professional can help you determine which one you have or whether simply to call it disordered eating.

First Two Steps for Healing an Eating Disorder

Step One: Find Providers

Eating disorders are best conquered with a team approach to address all aspects of you. Eating disorders are driven by unhealthy thoughts and thought patterns. It is imperative to seek mental health counseling to assist you in changing those thoughts. When we don't seek mental health counseling, all of the thoughts and experiences that contributed to the eating disorder don't get healed. Just like we seek providers who specialize in the specific needs of our physical bodies, seeking a mental health therapist who specializes in eating disorders for your mental health needs is essential.

Next, it is crucial to find a registered dietitian who also specializes in eating disorders. A dietitian will help guide you in establishing a healthy eating pattern, healthy food thoughts, and a healthy balance of foods. If you need to work on adjusting your weight, a dietitian will also guide you in weight adjustment. Both your dietitian and your mental health professional will be providing the support and counsel you need to reshape your thoughts and your relationship with food. Your dietitian will help you identify your ideal weight range and is skilled in guiding or coaching you along the way to achieving your ideal weight.

Your primary care physician is the third person you need on your team. Your primary care physician is an integral part of your journey. Your physician can evaluate your physical health and nutrition through lab work. Lab work can verify if you are getting enough fats, proteins, carbohydrates, vitamins, and minerals. Lab tests can also indicate if your body is not getting enough nutrients overall and whether that deficit is through food or a possible malabsorption condition. Your primary care physician can also recommend the weight range you should achieve for good health.

And yes, those weight charts really are accurate pertaining to minimum weight. Our bodies need a certain amount of nutrients, including vitamins, minerals, fats, and proteins. Trying to maintain good health at a caloric intake that is lower than what your body needs for your height will result in under-consumption of nutrients.

Even if you have worked with a registered dietitian in the past, if you are currently experiencing disordered eating, you need to work with one again. Invite them into your healing journey. The same goes for mental health help; invite a new therapist to work with you. Just as varied as each person is in the human race, each therapist will bring in new combinations of thoughts, perspectives, and expertise, and we can grow from those new perspectives. If you feel your connection with a provider of any kind is not serving your needs or goals, find a new provider or return to a previous provider who served you well.

Know that you are worth having providers you are comfortable with, you feel are competent, and who listen well to you. A good primary care physician will help you feel a solid foundation of care under your feet. Your primary care physician can also be your starting point as a source you can consult for referrals to find a registered dietitian and a mental health professional. You can also search online for these professionals.

Step Two: Dig In and Reach Out

Watching videos on YouTube by Natalie Forsythe was my first inspiration that eating disorders can be healed. Prior to that, I doubted mine could be healed and thought I was stuck in food anxieties forever. Natalie successfully healed from binge eating and was inspirational about the process. She shared it was not a quick process. Healing from an eating disorder can take years. That was a source of new hope for me in my new space of wanting to do what it takes to heal. My prior expectation had been that I was supposed to heal it quickly and get on with life; if I were unable to heal it quickly, it might not heal. I was now ready to take the time to heal the eating disorder. Any thoughts or emotions we are trying to heal can require patience because we are literally rewiring our brains, and that takes time.

In addition to watching Natalie Forsythe's videos, I searched online for articles about healing an eating disorder. One of the first suggestions I incorporated is to replace obsessive food thoughts with focusing on something you enjoy doing or that inspires you. I chose something simple that I could readily turn my attention to. I enjoy seeing something when it is freshly cleaned or tidied, including how it sparkles, shines, or looks organized. So, I practiced shifting my obsessive food thoughts to cleaning, organizing, or even simply planning a cleaning or organizing task.

Refocusing and shifting our thoughts helps our minds discover we can break our obsessive thought patterns instead of feeling stuck or chained by them. By choosing something that inspires us, we also begin to realize we can find joy, peace, and balance in life. We can start to feel healing progressing while knowing there is still much work to be done, thoughts to heal, and trust to build.

After spending some time shifting my obsessive food thoughts, I reached out to counseling online through Talkspace when I was forty-seven. When I first started reaching out for counseling, I did so because I had high anxiety and was overwhelmed, which was clouding my thinking, interrupting my sleep, and ultimately making my day-to-day functioning difficult. I had also requested a therapist experienced in eating disorders to try to begin addressing the issue with professional help. What I discovered was I needed to dig through some of the present anxieties before I could even reach the eating disorder.

I began to work with the Talkspace therapist on my anxiety, but I was not quite ready to make a concerted effort to address my food and weight thoughts. As I continued to work with my therapist, I wanted more and more to address the weight stronghold. I realized the weight issue required reframing the trio of body image, weight restriction, and food thoughts. I more strongly accepted that professional counsel really does help retrain unhealthy thought patterns into healthy ones.

The therapist suggested I work with a dietitian. I was reluctant because of the cost. Insurance only covers dietitians for diabetes and dialysis, and adding the cost of a dietitian on top of counseling seemed like a bit much. I hoped simply working with a mental health professional on mental and emotional challenges was enough. However, I knew the therapist was right, and out of curiosity, I did search the internet for a registered dietitian who specializes in eating disorders and works virtually. I contacted one I found in my search. I learned about her experience and that she uses the principles from the book *Intuitive Eating* by Evelyn Tribole and Elyse Resch as a foundation for her clients. This book is great inspirational reading for anyone who wants a healthy relationship with food; it teaches about the joyful and sustaining role food is intended to play in our lives. I told the dietitian I would get back to her when I was ready to start.

In the interim, I found a new family doctor. My wellness bloodwork showed small signs of malnutrition. Coupled with low BMI, the doctor recommended I work with a dietitian on weight gain. She was the first doctor who took a proactive approach of recommending steps, and it came at the time I was ready to receive it.

I believe the approach of having a doctor suggest a dietitian to a patient with a low BMI can be profitable, even if the patient is not ready to act upon it. The suggestion is a seed that keeps the need for weight gain alive. At some point in the future, the seed may bear fruit. The suggestion of weight gain, combined with the suggested action step of working with a dietitian, can give a person a more concrete approach. Only stating the patient needs to gain weight can leave the patient still too stuck in their own head with their fears.

I contacted the dietitian to get started, and I read *Intuitive Eating* before our first appointment. Reading the book was optional, but I was ready to be all in. At our initial consultation, we set up a monthly weight gain goal that we then broke down into weekly gains. Unless a person is at a dangerous weight or needs to adjust quickly for acute health needs, a gradual weight adjustment is ideal, giving both the body and the mind time to adapt and experience the change as normal. I worked with the dietitian for approximately a year and a half, gradually gaining weight and reshaping my relationship with food.

The Talkspace therapist I was working with was ready to go back to work in person, and she understandably needed to end her work with the Talkspace platform. After we ended, I took a few months to research which direction to go with counseling. I eventually turned to Psychology Today's provider search and found a psychologist licensed in Indiana, where I live, who specializes in eating disorders and embraced the option of virtual visits.

Your Healthy Relationship with Food

To establish a healthy relationship with food, you must include scientific knowledge about food and nutrition and pay intricate attention to your body. You have to learn what your hunger cues feel like. Hunger cues are those subtle and not-so-subtle signals our bodies give us to indicate when we need to eat. When you start to have that gnawing feeling in your stomach, it is getting close to the time to eat. If you go too long, your stomach will begin to growl, and/or your blood sugar will start to drop. Feeling dizzy or lightheaded, having difficulty focusing your thoughts, or feeling weak are indications your blood sugar is dropping too low and you have gone too long without eating. We do not want our blood sugar to drop too low because then our body's reaction when we put food in it is to spike the blood sugar up high in an effort to bring the body back into balance. We want blood sugar in a stable state because spiking sugar can cause damage to the body.

According to the American Psychological Association (APA), the hunger-fullness scale is an intuitive eating tool designed to help individuals get in touch with their hunger and fullness cues (American Psychological Association, 2020). The scale ranks our hunger and fullness cues from one to ten. Your goal is to eat between levels four and seven on the scale, which means you should start eating when you reach three or four on the scale and stop eating when you reach six or seven. It is essential to avoid reaching levels one or two and eight, nine, or ten because it may lead to making less-than-ideal food choices and potentially overeating. A Hunger/Fullness Scale diagram is included on the opposite page for your reference.

Because I had not been eating meals at regular intervals and had been eating most of my food at night, my body was not sending me hunger cues. My first step was to get my body used to eating three meals, and hopefully, it would start sending hunger cues.

I started with one-item breakfasts of fruit or protein and a small lunch, and I began to think about what evening foods I could move to other meals to disperse my calories more evenly throughout the day. Not only is an even distribution good for our energy levels, but it is good for our minds and, ultimately, our spirits. We want to break rigid food patterns and incorporate flexibility. Some days offer unintended variabilities in schedules or access to food, so we want to adapt to that change without sending our bodies into the fight-or-flight response. We can best adapt by developing a flexible mindset.

Gratefully, my hunger cues started working within a few days. I gradually added more foods to breakfast and lunch and used hunger cues to signal snacks. I achieved a steady, gradual weight gain and grew in appreciation of all foods and nutrients.

One particular nutrient that regained my appreciation was fat. Today, a lot of products emphasize that they are low fat and no fat. As someone who gravitated to extremes and viewed low this and low that—low weight, low fat, low cholesterol—as good, I began to think of "no fat" as best. The concept of *no fat* as being best is a skewed fallacy.

In addition to a healthy weight, our bodies need a healthy balanced amount of both fat and cholesterol. Our brains consist of 60 percent fat. To function well, our brains

HUNGER & FULLNESS
SCALE

Aim to stay within zones 4-7 as much as possible. Start eating when you reach 3-4 and stop when you reach 6-7. When you stop at 6, you will generally reach 7 within 15-20 minutes.

1 **Ravenous, faint & irritable**

2 **Very hungry, low energy, weak & dizzy**

3 **Hungry, distracted, irritable**

4 **Hungry, stomach growling**

5 **Starting to feel hungry**

6 **Satisfied, but can take a few more bites**

7 **Comfortably satisfied, can wait a few hours to eat again**

8 **Very full, probably ate a few bites beyond fullness**

9 **Stuffed, clothes feel tight**

10 **Overstuffed & feeling nauseous**

need omega-3 and omega-6 fatty acids that must be con-sumed through dietary sources because our bodies cannot make these. Omega fats also play a role in the health and maintenance of our central nervous system and retinas.

In addition to omega fats, our body also needs other fats, which brings us to the subject of cholesterol. Choles-terol plays a vital role in our bodies. It is essential for the formation of the cell walls of every cell in your body, for hormone production of some hormones, and for the pro-duction of bile acids, which are necessary for the absorp-tion of dietary fat and fat-soluble vitamins. Cholesterol also plays a part in synthesizing Vitamin D from the sun. Cholesterol that is too low can lead to malnourishment and also indicate to medical professionals that malnour-ishment is present.

Traditional labs establish their cholesterol ranges by averaging the levels of both healthy and unhealthy peo-ple. If we want to be healthy, we want to aim for the rang-es that foster health in our bodies. For healthy bodies, we should aim for optimal levels of cholesterol. Traditional labs generally say cholesterol levels between 120-199 are good. However, functional medicine standards say choles-terol levels should be between 150-200 for optimal health. I prefer to stay in the functional medicine guidelines since too little cholesterol can hinder the body. This was an im-portant factor for me because my cholesterol has been too low at times at 123, so I make a conscious effort to keep it above 150 by eating nuts and other healthy fats.

Breaking cholesterol down further, according to the American College of Cardiology and the American Heart Association, optimal levels of HDL (high-density lipopro-tein) cholesterol are greater than 60 mg/dL. HDL choles-terol is often referred to as "good" cholesterol because it helps remove LDL (low-density lipoprotein) cholesterol, or "bad" cholesterol, from the bloodstream.

Optimal levels of LDL cholesterol are less than 100 mg/dL. High levels of LDL cholesterol can contribute to the buildup of plaque in the arteries, increasing the risk of heart disease. It's important to note that optimal levels may vary depending on an individual's risk factors for heart disease. For example, individuals with a higher risk of heart disease or who have diabetes may need to have a goal of an LDL level less than 70 mg/dL.

A Few Mindset Tips

In establishing a healthy relationship with food, another key mindset is that no food is "bad." All foods are good and can be enjoyed in their proper proportions. Even a portion of those rich desserts, a delightful treat (if you like those), can be enjoyed. You are free to enjoy the foods you like. Just be sure to emphasize getting all the healthy nutrients, vitamins, and minerals your body needs, as well. If any specific dietary guidelines are present due to medical conditions, balance the foods you like with those guidelines in mind.

Another tip is it is important to eat foods that taste good to you. Going along with the principle in *Intuitive Eating* that all foods are good and can be enjoyed in proper proportions, taste is a factor that brings us pleasure in the foods we eat. While it can bring pleasure, it can also bring displeasure, and we can pay attention to both factors. I was regularly eating raw kale because I had heard kale is very good for the body. When I learned you should eat foods that taste good to you, I stopped, evaluated kale, and realized I honestly do not like raw kale. However, just because we do not like a food one way does not mean it has to be banished from our diet because foods prepared a different way might be enjoyable. After taking a break from kale, I tried other methods and discovered I like the flavor of kale when it is roasted or cooked. When it is raw,

I like it topped with mustard or salsa. So now I can have kale back and can reap the benefits of its nutrient profile.

Did you know you need to eat fats with a salad to absorb its nutrients? I was intrigued to discover it is a necessity to prepare salads with some kind of fat in order for your body to absorb the fat-soluble vitamins in the vegetables. I like the flavor of lettuce by itself so, for years, I ate salads with no dressing. But when I discovered that fats boost nutrient absorption, I realized fat-laden salad dressings are good for salads, and people have been doing it right by adding fats. I still have not used salad dressing much because I enjoy the fun and creativity of finding other fat sources for my salads, such as cottage cheese, nuts, or seeds.

Since we have covered BMI in this chapter, I'd like to take the opportunity to discuss views of BMI for those who may face the challenge of having a BMI higher than the levels recommended on BMI charts. In the Health at Every Size (HAES) approach, individuals who face no medical problems due to excess weight are encouraged to focus on balanced eating, proper proportions, and movement or exercise. This approach can reduce weight stigma and provide better long-term results with improved health through balanced eating and exercise. If interested, consult with your medical provider and a dietitian specializing in HAES to see if this approach is right for you.

I want to share my story right down to the core of healing because the truth is what set me free, and other people who find the truth inside them will be set free, too. Sometimes, we need to find the truth in small increments because the whole picture at once will overwhelm us emotionally or make it difficult for our minds to understand. Sometimes the degree of depth a person needs to go to heal will be less or more than someone else's depth. As with the entirety of life, healing is an individual work that is completely unique in the finite details. We can gain inspiration, guidance, and direction from others who have gone through similar situations, and we can get advice from medical professionals and mental health practitioners about things that can help, but we are the only ones who can apply the advice or sense what is or is not working. Inner work is a picture only you can paint and a song only you can write and sing.

Any details I share of hard events and the unhealthy thoughts that resulted reveal how we can pave paths with thoughts that don't lead us to roads of truth, light, and goodness. We encounter dark spots where the lights go out, but we can turn those lights back on.

Discussion

1. What are some things you can do to move into a place of readiness to hear the inner voice within you?

_____

_____

_____

_____

2. What foods that you dislike could you try preparing another way to see if you like them? For example, you may not like broccoli, but you find broccoli covered with cheese to be delicious.

_____

_____

_____

_____

3. What additional fat sources can you put on your salads?

_____

_____

_____

_____

4. Are you within a healthy weight range according to weight charts?

_____

_____

_____

_____

5. Do you have obsessive thoughts about food, such as thinking about it when you are not hungry, keeping your-

self busy so you will not think of food, or feeling fear if you do think of food like, "Oh no, I'm not supposed to be thinking about food?" If so, are you ready to be free?

_____

_____

_____

_____

6. If you have obsessive food thoughts, what fun activities or hobbies could you focus on when those obsessive food thoughts come up?

_____

_____

_____

_____

7. What other steps are you ready to take to heal those thoughts and change those thought patterns?

_____

_____

_____

_____

8. What foods have you previously thought were *bad*, but you now realize are good when consumed in proper proportions?

_____

_____

_____

_____

9. If you face the challenge of a high BMI, would you like to consider the Health at Every Size approach? What benefits or drawbacks might this approach offer you?

_____

_____

_____

_____

Poems

Feel It Raining

Feel it raining,
And you are free.
The clouds are lifted,
And now you see.

The sun is shining.
It's a brand-new day.
The place is familiar;
That's what you can say.

The rooms have been swept.
The dust is gone.
You see some bright colors,
And you hear a new song.

Then you look closely
To see, and behold,
Just past the shutters,
You see precious gold.

No Longer Hide

May we no longer hide ourselves
From the beauty that we are.
May we no longer stand and mock
Our flaws from afar.

May we reverently draw near
To self and see
The treasure chest
Inside of us,
Find the lock,
And turn the key.

Chapter 3
Unveiling Trauma

A T A YOUNG AGE, PERHAPS as a result of the accident, I decided I would not have a victim mentality. I would be strong and brave, and in my young mind, that meant not sharing my struggles. This mindset was one of the thought patterns that helped drive me into perfectionism. When we feel we can't express our weaknesses or fears, we become isolated. By telling ourselves we need to be strong all the time or that we are required to be fear-free every moment, we create an internal environment of shame because we are working to ignore our challenges and fears instead of addressing them and identifying the needs they point to. Shame produces anxiety and confusion.

I have discovered I'm a person who more readily looks at where I am and how I go forward than where I've been. Deep down within me lies a sense of awe and wonder for life. In the past, I felt I needed to hold it at a distance because the uncertainty of dreams, wonder, and curiosity felt frightening; I rejected the truths of the things I possibly could not change. The uncertainty of not knowing what I could not change or how to navigate into the future were hard to bear, so I spent my energy focusing on things that were certain and that I could control through the means of perfectionism and an eating disorder. An eating disorder operates the same as other addictions. Addictions are coping tools that help us cope with the uncertainties life is filled with. As human beings, we want certainty. However, building cognitive flexibility to replace the intolerance of uncertainty will lead to better mental health.

As I began to heal my eating disorder, I started to let go of that need to feel in control. My dietitian was the first person who pointed out that I had the valuable trait of curiosity. When I first began working with her, she stated she was confident I would do well because I had curiosity. I paused and realized I appreciated that trait within myself. Curiosity opens up the excitement of exploration, dreaming, and imagining possibilities.

In the past, I had beheld curiosity, awe, and wonder from a space outside of my truest self because I was trying to push them away. I was not accessing and living in the same space as my deepest being. One day early in 2023, I stepped into an even deeper appreciation of these traits when I was introduced to Marianne Williamson's famous quote, often titled "Our Deepest Fear." The first few lines read:

"Our deepest fear is not that we are inadequate. Our deepest fear is that we are powerful beyond measure. It is our light, not our darkness, that most frightens us."

The moment I read the passage, a light came on for me. It revealed the power of the wonder that lay inside of me. In that moment, I knew one of my lights was my awe, my wonder, my curiosity, and my creativity. It is a light that glows, fills, and inspires me inside. It was then that I grasped the joy of knowing my light and the gift of the valuable trait. I've learned to walk in the same space as wonder. In this place of awe and wonder, I reach into the depths of my being and drink from my deepest wells, and I bring out creativity.

If I were to sum up my mental state during all the years I had the eating disorder, it would be a state of confusion. That confusion also led to a lack of trust. I did not trust myself. I believed, as we often do in the Christian community, that a stronger trust in God would solve all of my problems, confusion, and insecurities. "Just trust God," we Christians often say. But we have to get to the heart of the problem. Trusting God was not the heart of my problem.

After the accident, I did not look back and wish I was not disabled. I looked at where I was at present and how I could go forward. My truest reality is that God, my Source and my Creator, has walked with me all along the way. He has revealed himself to me through his comfort and care in the difficult times, and he has rejoiced with me in the good times. His goodness has followed me all the days of my life.

When my Talkspace therapist suggested I might be affected by trauma, I thought that was impossible because I had put everything about the accident behind me and gone forward. I was fine. *Other people are affected by trauma, but not me; trauma is too dramatic,* I thought.

As I sat down to write this book, wanting to explain my conception of drama and trauma, I had to turn to sources first to define the two. Because of their similarities both phonetically and functionally, they kept overlapping in my mind. The Center for Health Care Strategies defines *trauma* as the lasting adverse effects on an individual's mental, physical, social, emotional, or spiritual well-being as the result of exposure to an incident or series of emotionally disturbing events. *The Merriam-Webster Dictionary* defines *drama* as a situation involving an interesting or intense conflict of forces. Amid my efforts to remain brave and strong, I had cut off my ability to view the drama in my life and its tender spots because I had blocked out self-compassion.

When trauma is not processed through to a healthy endpoint, it gets stuck in our subconscious minds and can keep our nervous systems in a stress response mode, or fight, flight, or freeze. "The body keeps the score," as Bessel van der Kolk eloquently states in his book with that phrase for its title.

Trauma is an emotional and psychological response. What has created trauma for one person may not produce trauma for someone else. An individual's perception determines emotional trauma, and perception depends on how we experience and react to the event. We create struggle and confusion within ourselves when we minimize trauma.

I minimized the drama and was unaware of the trauma, so I wanted nothing to do with claiming those in my life. I wanted to be brave and strong. I had determination and resilience, but I neglected the tender spots. Our tender spots become wounds and weaknesses when we neglect them, but they become strengths when we tend to them with compassion and heal them.

Once I became able, within the last few years, to have compassion for myself and tend to my own grief and vulnerability, I understood and responded better to others' suffering and sadness. Because I had blocked self-compassion and attempted to prohibit myself from addressing grief from hardships or showing vulnerability, I struggled to know how to respond to drama, grief, and vulnerability in others. On social media, I told people to look on the bright side or that all would be better before long. While on the one hand, I wished people could *get over it* like I told myself to do, on the other hand, I knew we were supposed to have compassion for others, and I was hesitant about the detachment of my wishes and statements. I tried to comprehend compassion with my head, but my heart could not entirely and consistently draw near to compassion for others until I broke through to compassion for myself. Then, I understood compassion.

Compassion is the sympathetic concern for suffering with the motivation to relieve that suffering. We often focus on compassion as something we feel for others. We also need to have compassion for ourselves—the sympathetic concern for our own suffering with the motivation to relieve our distress.

When we feel our response to someone else's suffering is too cold, we should ask ourselves, "Why is this triggering an aloof reaction in me?" When we get to the bottom of our adverse reactions and judgments, we can replace them with empathy and compassion. With empathy, we join in, understand, and share in others' feelings; with compassion, we experience our own feelings that arise when we see another person's suffering, and we feel motivated to relieve that suffering. The term "moved with compassion" derives from the fact that compassion includes impetus to alleviate suffering. Compassion inspires action.

Trauma and Core Beliefs

During physical recovery from an accident and hospital stays, a person may experience separation from loved ones, which the subconscious mind may interpret as abandonment. Abandonment is a subjective emotional state in which a person feels left behind, neglected, insecure, or unsafe. Abandonment trauma occurs when a person feels or perceives any type of abandonment that is extremely painful to them. Given a child's limited cognitive and emotional development, because the brain at that age has not yet fully developed the skills of reasoning and emotional intelligence, children may interpret unintentional abandonment as a traumatic event. Children take their experiences as truth and don't possess a full enough perspective on life to process them. In this way, a child innocently takes on ideas that aren't true as core beliefs because they perceive them as true. Core beliefs are firmly held beliefs, consistent over time, that affect a person's worldview and self-perception.

The pain of separation occurred most strongly for me during my stay at the Rehabilitation Institute of Chicago. It was a vital and valuable step for my physical recovery, but I was there in Chicago five days a week without family, so I missed them. My parents came on Friday evenings to take me home for the weekend, and we returned on Sunday afternoon. My stay at RIC was during winter. A few times, there was too much snow for my parents to make the trip to bring me home. The news that they were not coming those weeks was heartbreaking. Today's atmosphere in pediatric care includes all the advancements in mental health knowledge since 1976. Professionals pay even more attention to emotional health through counseling and activities that specifically address coping with the stress of being in the hospital or rehabilitation care while away from loved ones.

Emotional Support and Care

Most hospitals now have a team of medical professionals dedicated to providing emotional support for children. These professionals typically include trained therapists, social workers, and other mental health professionals. These specialists help provide emotional support through counseling, support groups, and play therapy. Counseling offers a safe and supportive space for children to express their feelings and discuss their challenges. Support groups allow pediatric patients to connect with others who face similar experiences, and play therapy helps children better express themselves and their feelings. Play therapy can help a child process their emotions and understand why they may feel a certain way.

Hospitals have also begun to use art therapy to help pediatric patients process and understand their emotions. Children can creatively express themselves through artistic activities like drawing or painting. Art therapy can help them understand their feelings better while also allowing them to explore others' feelings.

In addition, hospitals often provide educational programs for parents and caregivers to help them understand their children's challenges and how to best support them. Many hospitals also have programs that offer support for families dealing with long-term medical problems. These programs may assist with financial issues, transportation, home care services, and information and support resources. They may also offer support groups or special events for families to allow them to connect with others in similar circumstances.

Preventing Emotional Trauma

Three keys to navigating traumatic events without the event causing emotional trauma are human connections, support, and coping skills. Human connection gives us a sense of belonging, comfort, and backing that allows us to feel seen, heard, and respected. Having solid relationships with others will enable us to feel more secure and fulfilled. This connection can also help us to challenge ourselves and get through difficulties because we have someone to back us up and provide encouragement. In tough times, comfort and support are invaluable.

The emotional support that comes through both human connection and practical aid assists people through complex events. A few good methods of practical aid to support people in difficult situations are bringing meals, taking care of housework, yard work, or snow removal, helping them gather information and resources, and assisting them in getting to appointments. These are essential ways to support them to lighten their load physically and mentally. The stress of complex events can hinder the frontal lobe functioning of our brains, reducing our abilities to think clearly to complete tasks and make decisions. So, your assistance truly is a gift. The next time you support someone through a difficult period, you can identify the aid that will be helpful for them and know that your care is a gift.

As mentioned above, stress, which aborts our feeling of safety, also hinders the functioning of the frontal lobes in our brains. Without clear thoughts, we don't feel safe. Safety is found through peace. One way to foster peace is through coping skills.

Developing Coping Skills

Developing coping skills is essential for building inner strength and resilience. Coping skills can fall into categories such as emotional coping, problem-based coping, and avoidance coping. Emotional coping involves managing emotional distress. Problem-based coping focuses on tackling the situation by finding solutions and creating action plans. Healthy avoidance coping is intended to provide temporary relief from stress.

Emotional coping involves working through emotions when you cannot change the outcome, such as a loved one's death or the passage of time. Problem-based coping includes taking actions to bring a change or make a difference in a situation, such as making an appointment to talk to a doctor about a concern or contacting the plumber to fix the faucet.

Healthy avoidance coping, or avoidance-focused coping, is the act of avoiding distressing emotions with the intent of returning to face them later. It includes taking a break from a difficult emotion and returning to address it at a more manageable time. Examples include taking a ten-minute break or going for a walk to cool down and clear your mind.

Unhealthy avoidance is the kind of avoidance we are trying to heal through the tools in this book. It includes avoiding emotions, burying them, and not returning to address them. Examples include overeating or undereating, dulling emotions through excessive exercise, or deflecting anxiety by playing games on your cell phone to avoid your needed task.

A few helpful coping skills we can learn to practice are identifying our triggers, noticing our bodies, journaling, praying, and naming our emotions. These skills are practical for both children and adults. They are especially valuable skills to teach children so they are empowered with a lifetime of benefits, and the skills will bring healing and renewal to adults. Let's take a look at these skills.

Identifying Triggers

By identifying our triggers, we can anticipate situations that cause us distress and develop strategies to manage them effectively. My friend Paul had misophonia, a condition where one or more common sounds cause an intense emotional response such as disgust, anger, distress, or panic. His triggers were his cats bathing themselves and loud human food chewing or lip-smacking sounds. His responses were disgust and anger. The anger was only in the moment; as soon as the sound stopped, his anger did, too.

Neuropsychologist Pawel Jastreboff identified misophonia as a disorder in 2001. Studies on misophonia have
identified the possibility of a physiological disruption in
the neural pathway of sound processing and the possibility
of the disorder being initiated by a trauma response. Over
time, through self-administered use of the CBT method of
changing his thoughts, Paul reduced the intensity of his
irritation regarding his cats' bathing.

Paul would often gently remind himself that his cats'
bathing sounds were not their fault, and that bathing is
what cats do by nature. He also convinced himself the
sound would soon stop, and all would be well. He simply
began to pause what he was doing if he was in the midst of
something that required concentration when he got triggered by their sounds. He waited until the sound ceased
because he knew that was the best way to honor himself
and his task instead of trying to force himself to concen-
trate. He knew his brain was in the fight-or-flight response
at the moment, and trying to force concentration would
create more anxious thoughts and turn up the intensity of
his stress response. If the sound seemed like it was going
to continue for a while, he would turn on some music.

If human eating sounds triggered Paul's misophonia
reaction, he would either endure them or leave the room.
If the person knew him well, he would sometimes inform
them of his trigger, and they would mutually decide their
best plan. He discovered that many people responded
with understanding and made a conscious effort to eat
quietly or were not offended if he excused himself from
the room.

In any situation, identifying your triggers and determining your best response is an excellent method for reducing your stress response. A parent who gets overstim-
ulated by a crying infant can identify their best coping
strategy. If a coworker repeatedly irritates you, you can

plan your response for the next time it happens. If a child gets angry when a sibling wants to play with their toy, we can gently teach them the value of sharing.

When one of Paul's cats passed away, and he was no longer handling the strained feline relationship the two cats had shared, he discovered his remaining cat's loud bathing sounds barely bothered him any longer. In fact, he now cherished every sound his kitty made. He discovered that handling the strained relationship between his two cats had added a level of stress that must have been housed in his subconscious mind and he had been unaware of how to process it. When the sad event of losing his beloved pet occurred, leaving him with one kitty instead of two, the natural process of the hidden stress being lifted and him now cherishing his second kitty confirmed further for Paul that we have many unknowns about ourselves that we have yet to discover. The situation also reminded Paul that with gentle self-compassion, we can continue to learn and grow.

Noticing Your Body

Bringing our attention to our bodies can have a soothing effect that calms our nervous system and our minds. By directing our attention to our bodies, we center ourselves by reminding our conscious and subconscious minds that we are here in the now. There are several ways to do this. We can be creative and play with different techniques.

Start with a simple mental body scan with breathing. Begin at the top of your head and, in your mind, slowly scan down each part of your body, noticing any pains, sensations, or muscle tightness. Do the parts feel light or heavy? If you are sitting, notice the weight of your body on the chair at all the points of contact. Notice the weight of your feet on the floor. Then, take a deep breath in and notice where you feel the breath. Do you feel it most in your nose, chest, or belly? Continue to breathe three more breaths, focusing on the sensation. Next, slowly bring your awareness back to your surroundings. When you are done, observe how you feel. Do you feel calmer? If you just did a body scan while reading this text and felt it did nothing for you, don't give up. The scan is more effective when you can do it without having to focus on reading the instructions. After doing it a few times, you will have it memorized. Numerous videos and apps are available to guide you in body scans. You can find many on YouTube and elsewhere.

You can vary body scans by changing the number of breaths you take or the body parts you focus on. In some scans, just observe your body. If you discover you are slouching, don't adjust your posture; just observe. At other times, use the scan to align your body and correct the slouching posture or tilting head. Be creative with your scans.

Another exercise for body awareness is to notice where you feel your emotions. Our emotions bring sensations to our bodies. When you are angry, do you feel it in your chest, throat, or hands? When you have anxiety, where do you feel the sensations? Where do you feel compassion?

These body awareness exercises can also reward us by getting to know ourselves. Knowing ourselves brings richness to life. We can more fully share all the richness within. We can also more accurately manage and fully experience our emotions.

Journaling

Journaling is a technique that unlocks insight into ourselves. When we write down our thoughts, we can stand back and look objectively at situations and discover thoughts we did not know were present in our minds.

When we let the thoughts flow out, things sometimes make more sense.

In my tenth-grade English class, we were assigned to keep a journal for several weeks. The teacher gave us topics to write about. I enjoyed the process, but I never thought to make journaling a regular practice. I did not hear much more about journaling until the last several years. Then it first struck me as odd that I did not journal over the years, given how much I like to write. Not downright odd, though, because I know part of me simply did not want to take the time to write; I felt there were better uses of my time. I did not see the wisdom of having journals I might never read again or diaries stored away in closets or sitting on shelves. Tablets of thoughts and notes, to me, after a while, feel like clutter, and I throw them away.

However, the power of journaling can be found in the act of writing itself by getting those thoughts out of our heads and down onto paper. Journals do not even have to be retained. What you write can be thrown away immediately or saved for however short or long you deem appropriate. That said, some people keep their journals and reference them when they write books or have used their journal entries as the book's entire content. Tablets of journaled thoughts will no longer feel like clutter to me.

Journaling is becoming more popular now that more attention has been brought to it. People are realizing the power they can tap into by pouring their thoughts onto paper. Take ten minutes to write about your thoughts, whether good thoughts, thoughts of stress you want to overcome, or problems you want to solve. Getting our thoughts down on paper (or a computer screen) helps us get them out of our heads and brings more order to them, allowing us to see solutions we did not see before or to find more peace through identifying our thoughts and allowing ourselves to take another look at them. Scientists say journaling on paper can enhance recall because writing activates more areas of the brain, and the tactile sensation of the paper can increase emotional processing. Whether you use computer or pen and paper, the best method is the one that works for you.

Prayer

Prayer has been a cherished privilege in my life. I'll focus here on prayer as a coping mechanism. Belief in a Higher Power, a power outside of ourselves, gives us strength to endure the hard things in life. Back in school, the many times I fell down, I could always find God's comforting presence through my faith in him, and I silently thanked him each time for keeping me safe.

Is prayer simply a mental health technique? It is that and more. It is an avenue of mental and spiritual connection to our Higher Power. Whether our need is small or it is dire, through belief and prayer, we can find the strength to make it through our challenging moments. Outside of praying during our own hard moments or petitioning for help with others' challenges, prayer offers us a connection with our Source of Life through the expression of gratitude or through simply listening in the stillness for the voice of our Creator.

When my corneal specialist performed my first superficial keratectomy on my right eye in 2022, he encouraged me by saying that most patients forego sedation and complete the surgery with numbing only. After all, the procedure only takes a few minutes. He discovered my eye took longer. A few months later, when we were going to do the same procedure on my left eye, he offered sedation. I declined, telling him I liked to observe. I was fascinated during the first surgery on the right eye when I observed the vast difference in clarity of vision as he peeled off the intruding tissue. The day of the second surgery, my mind must have been tuned to a different setting because, although a shorter surgery, I became more anxious. While he was working, I resorted to prayer as I wondered how my mind would endure those few minutes of tissue-scraping sounds I did not recall hearing during the first surgery. I simply prayed, "Lord, you're going to have to help me through this." And he did.

Naming Emotions

A couple of years ago, I was introduced to the strategy of naming our emotions. Identifying and naming our emotions empowers us to grasp our feelings and take the appropriate mental steps to handle them. I had not realized I did not have a grip on this skill, nor had I ever put thought into the effectiveness of welcoming and dissipating emotions that this tool brings. Depending on what source you consult, there are six to eight core emotions. Often, we can even more specifically name the emotions we are feeling that fall into these categories.

A helpful visual device is the emotions wheel, first developed by American psychologist Robert Plutchick in 1980. Plutchick identified eight core emotions, but the wheel has since been adapted into many different versions to use as a tool to bring awareness to emotions. I like to use a version that includes love as one of the core emotions since love is at the root of life.

The wheel helps us to simplify the act of identifying the emotions we are experiencing. This process can be especially helpful when we face challenging or confusing times. We can look at the wheel and first identify the core emotion we are feeling and then trace out further to its sub-emotions to see if any of those identify our emotions more precisely. Then, we can proceed to identify what sparked that emotion, what mental and physical response was created by the emotion, and what action we took in response to the emotion. Being aware of our emotions and our responses to them helps us to share and express them in a constructive way. We can also analyze their role in our lives, which allows us to adjust ourselves to the things we desire and the outcomes that interest us. We can then cultivate the emotional states that help us work toward our goals.

I have included here an emotions wheel to use to help name emotions. This wheel is not all-inclusive—many more emotions can be named—but it can give us a starting point. Regularly naming emotions soothes our minds because it gives us clarity and helps us to understand our feelings. We can teach ourselves that we are in charge of our emotions. Emotions don't have to just happen to us. We can be in charge of them and befriend them. We do not want to stuff them down and try to make them go away. We want to acknowledge them and learn what they are trying to teach us. Emotions can guide us to who we are when we learn how to listen and respond to them in healthy ways.

Emotions are messengers. When we are examining emotions and what they are trying to teach us, it is helpful to note that emotions are energy moving in and through our bodies. Emotions are a chemical response in our bodies, and according to former Harvard brain scientist Dr. Jill Bolte Taylor, the chemical response takes ninety seconds to run through the body. Dr. Taylor goes on to say that any remaining emotional response is due to a person choosing to stay in that emotion through thoughts. In other words, if we did not choose to continue to think about the emotion or situation that triggered it, we could let the emotion go.

The ninety-second rule is helpful in managing our emotions. We benefit when we can let the emotion run

The Emotions Wheel

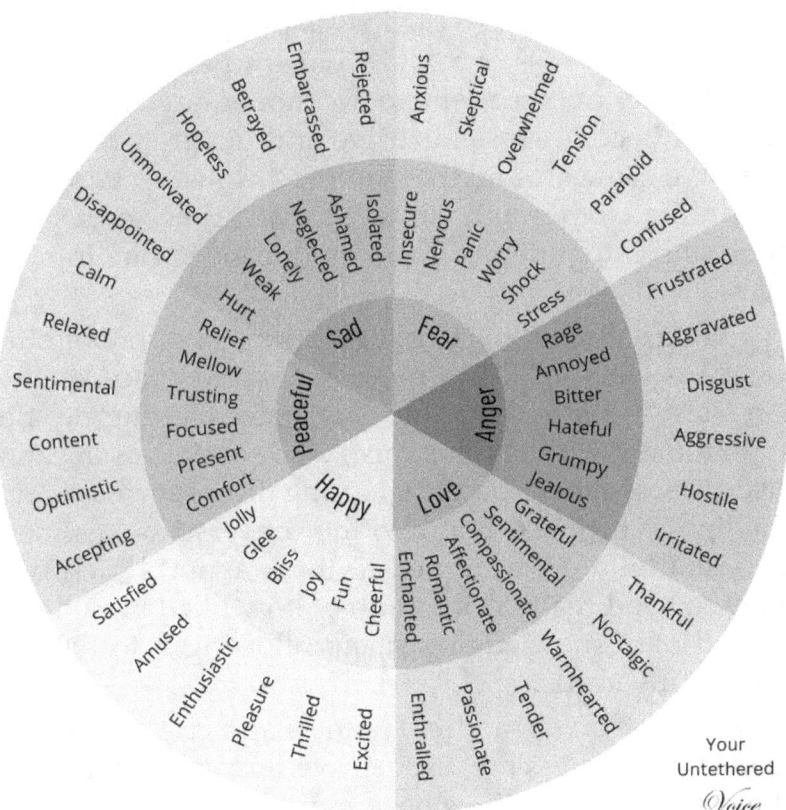

Your
Untethered
Voice

through, name it, and objectively evaluate it. Let's look at some emotions and what they can be telling us.

Sadness, Grief, and Depression

Sadness tells us we are experiencing loss or grief, and we need to let go of something. That something may be a goal, a dream, a relationship, a mindset, or a belief system. Grief, furthermore, indicates we need to be heard, comforted, or our grief needs to be validated.

Minor griefs, like skinning your knee, usually resolve quickly without long-term effects. More profound emotional griefs or losses may not go away, and they require adaptation and healing in accepting our loss. These griefs are permanent because the loss is permanent. When we experience the loss of a loved one—a permanent loss— the intensity of our grief usually moderates over time as the grief becomes less intrusive and integrated into our lives. We grow around the grief, and we wrap it in softer swaddling clothes and allow it to take times of rest. We build and integrate the honor of our loved one into our lives.

Perhaps life calls us to integrate the honor of our other losses, as well. All losses possess a sacred space, and we can learn to place them into that space. During my first appointment with my therapist, who specializes in eating disorders, she mentioned that eating disorders mask grief. She lightly dropped that into the conversation, as therapists skillfully do, as a seed to think about. I picked up that seed and realized the truth of how I had buried grief instead of acknowledging it and allowing it to help me address my needs.

When we do not address sadness and grief, it can hang around as depression. Even if we are not experiencing clinical depression, if we have sadness that we repress, it will detract from our ability to move forward in full expression and discovery of our abilities because that unaddressed need in our sadness creates a wound that requires our unconscious resources to tend to.

I have discovered helpful insight recently in my mission to lean into emotions to hear their message. When thoughts in my head or words coming out of my mouth cause me to get choked up, getting choked up is our body's signal that we need to address something. Grief, as well as joy, can choke us up. We will know in that moment whether we are experiencing grief or joy. If grief, we can give attention to it and grow stronger. If joy, we can let joy flow and celebrate it. In either case, we can thank our bodies for giving us that extra signal to address our needs or joys.

Anxiety

Anxiety tells us we need to face something. Anxiety is triggered by thoughts about the past, present, or future. When I'm feeling anxious, I've learned to stop and ask myself, "Why am I feeling this way?" For present-time situations, triggers can be something big like running late for an appointment or something small like there is a big, black, speedy spider crawling on my wall. In each instance, I can ask myself, "What steps can I take in this situation, and how can I calm my anxiety?"

If I am running late for an appointment, I may be able to contact the other party and tell them I'll be late. At the same time, if I cannot contact them, I can reassure myself that this will not end in catastrophe and that I will be safe. I'll still be alive, and appointments can be rescheduled if need be. In the case of the spider, I can end its life, try to capture it and put it outside, or let it continue on its journey and appreciate the tasks it performs for nature. (I usually allow it to continue on its journey unless it is getting too close to crawling on me.)

Anxiety about the past tells us there are emotions we need to address and resolve. We can address those through thought or discussion with a friend or therapist. Anxiety about the future tells us we are feeling unprepared and fearing the unknown. We can take steps to gather information or take actions to help us feel more prepared for the future. An expectant mother may feel unprepared to care for her new baby. She can go to classes for expectant mothers, read books on the subject, and talk to other women who have faced the same fears. When my eye surgeries were coming up, I read about the procedures and talked to people in an online support group who had been through the same procedure. I took steps to prepare meals ahead of time for the recovery period. I also stocked my nightstand with some bottled natural fruit-flavored water to help soothe and comfort me through recovery. I learned from my therapist that incorporating soothing, pampering factions into our difficult times is a simple tool that helps ease the anxiety of our trying times. Soothing commodities could be flavored water, audiobooks, podcasts, or a favorite food.

The key to anxiety is it is triggered by fear. We do not feel safe. We need to find the information, thoughts, and actions that will help us return to a feeling of safety.

Another method of dealing with anxiety is to recognize our anxiety is our mind's way of highlighting that we care about something. For example, if we are nervous about an upcoming photo shoot, when we inquire within, we may discover it is because these pictures are for an important event, and we want to capture our best shot.

That describes me when I did the photo shoot for my author's pictures for this book. I had talks with myself that morning to calm my nervousness while I was getting ready. Because we are anxious when we care about something, we can say, "I'm anxious about X because I care about Y." When I told myself I was anxious because I cared, I immediately felt the softness of the compassion soothe the nervousness, and it transformed the anxiety into joyful anticipation.

Anger

Anger indicates we to need address or let go of something. Anger is always accompanied by another emotion. It signals the presence of an underlying feeling, such as sadness, betrayal, or fear. Addressing both of the emotions will equip you with wisdom and insight for your future encounters with anger.

When we become angry because we are trying to open a jar and are hindered by our hand that does not function fully, beneath the anger lies sadness. To address that sadness, we have to acknowledge it is there, let go of our belief that our hand should function wholly at this moment, and have the patience to keep trying via our present method or find another method.

We can also examine anger as a motivator. For a person who could improve their hand function through therapy, anger could motivate them to do therapy. Processing the anger and recognizing it is being transformed into positive motivation is empowering. The person whose hand will not improve with therapy is motivated to polish self-compassion, acceptance, and patience.

For years, I told myself that trying to open a stubborn jar with limited use of one of my hands did not make me angry. Self-regulation of anger ruled, and I was able to find solutions, so I stuffed the anger down without acknowledging it because anger gets labeled as bad. Anger is not bad, and it is not our enemy—it is a friendly messenger that tells us something needs to be addressed. By stuffing anger down and pushing it away, we are hindering its ability to send us messages about other things in our lives, too. Thereby, we are creating yet another avenue of losing touch with ourselves. Even if our present incident is easily solved, denying anger dulls its voice and endangers us by letting the hard things of life walk all over us.

An example of anger with underlying betrayal is a parent feeling betrayed by a child coming home after curfew when the parent had trusted their child to be on time. Another example of when we may feel anger and betrayal is when we depend on someone scheduled to come to aid us, and they do not arrive. Many people depending on home health care through the presently short-staffed system encounter times when the caregiver does not arrive. We hear many stories of friends, family, or people in the community who experience this, and they are caught in situations with the person in need at home by themselves or a loved one having to call off work at the last minute.

An example of anger with underlying fear is a person angry because of fear of declining mobility. They are angry because they fear they cannot play a part in stopping the decline. And angry because they feel they cannot find the help they need. This was me. Solving my anger and fear required me to evaluate my beliefs and emotions. As with other emotions, anger may be signaling we need to let go of an idea or belief system.

When I let go of my belief that walking independently was the only acceptable method of mobility for me, I was set free to experience peace and released to devote energy to pursuing the passions of creativity within me. I discovered forms of creativity within me I had never known were present because I had not taken the time to recognize or explore them. I had been devoting my cognitive energy to everything it took to resist other methods of mobility.

My anger and fear were also accompanied by frustration. Frustration indicates you are being stifled, being unheard, or are internalizing (not sharing) your thoughts and emotions. When we are frustrated, we need to reach out and share our thoughts, address our internal needs, and find the people who can listen and help.

As I began to look at my thoughts, I recalled my reflection as a teenager that if I had to choose between mental function and mobility, I would choose mental function. My mobility was good then, so the thought got tucked away in my mind. Next, I began to look objectively at my adult life experiences with physical therapy; the fact was therapy made me feel overwhelmed. I decided if I were going to pursue therapy, I'd have to find methods and loads that would work for me. Finally, I had to look at my fear. Why did I fear mobility decline?

As I looked deeper, I welcomed further investigation of the thought that popped up in my mind from time to time that some people spend years, even lifetimes, using a walker or wheelchair for mobility. Many of them live fulfilling lives, so why couldn't I? I realized I could. Whether I walk independently, walk with a walker, or use a wheelchair, I can still live a fulfilling life. Walking independently does provide the most ease in daily life, travel, and everywhere else you can think of, but the use of a walking aid or wheelchair supplies the same value to life with accommodations and forethought. Walking aids and wheelchairs do require planning. That fact emphasizes the importance of mental health and fulfilling relationships for users because the ability to thrive mentally will allow them to keep climbing mountains and resting upon summits.

The frustrations faced with disability give disabled persons opportunities to choose to become angry and bitter, repress anger, or release it. We can all, whether disabled or not, examine our opportunities to let go of anger. Holding onto anger can be tempting because anger gives a false sense of power. The truth is you're not being fair to yourself when you hold on to the anger and hinder yourself from being the true you. Being the true you only comes from living in wholeness. Anger will hold you hostage. The goodness of the world wants you to be free.

Envy

Envy teaches us that we want to set goals. We see something we want to achieve. Envy is a mirror that allows us to turn the light back upon ourselves to see within and reach for more. We can then plan the steps to reach our goals. This planning and reflection also gives us the opportunity to evaluate circumstances and accept what we cannot change or to tweak our goal into something that can be achieved.

Take, for example, Satavia, who envied her cousin because she had a larger house. Satavia looked within herself and discovered that she would enjoy owning a larger house. She had learned if we envy someone because they have a larger house, we can recognize that we would like to have one. She knew she would have to increase her income to buy a larger house. Satavia identified her options as getting more education, securing a higher salary by requesting a salary increase, making a job change, or becoming an entrepreneur to increase her income. Satavia secured a pay raise and also took courses to increase her skills. She now owns her dream house and is considering starting a side business to see where it takes her.

Happiness and Joy

Happiness teaches us to savor the moment and be present in it. Its cousin, joy, teaches us that something wants to be celebrated. The next time you feel happy, take time to be present. If that time is now, then be present right now. The next time you feel joy, celebrate the thing bringing you joy. For example, if it's your child graduating from high school or college, celebrate!

Fear

Fear tells us there is something we need to do or accept. If we fear losing the ability to walk, we either strengthen the muscles and neural pathways to continue walking or we accept the use of mobility aids. Those are the two peaceful choices we have. If it is not possible to continue walking, we are left with one peaceful choice. Continuing to engage with fear robs us of peace and power and hinders us from accurately loving ourselves and others. Christianity teaches us

"For God has not given us a spirit of fear, but one of power, love, and sound judgment."

— 2 Timothy 1:7, CSB

To apply that truth, we need to identify what we fear and take action to do or accept the things we need to so we can address that fear.

If we fear poor grades in school, we study and turn in assignments, or we accept poor grades. If we fear having surgery, we find out more information about the procedure and precautions, or we choose not to have the surgery and accept the alternatives. Not every fear will be simple to solve or address. Life bears many uncertainties and many complex situations, but the truth that we can address the emotion of fear will bring us peace.

Our job is to learn how to manage each emotion and respond to our emotions' messages. We can respond to the messages of our emotions by pausing and asking ourselves what our feelings are here to teach us. We do not have to be ruled by our emotions; rather, when we partner with them, we benefit from their instruction and continue making new discoveries about ourselves.

Healing Trauma

The key to healing trauma is to calm the mind and feel safe. Trauma puts our bodies into the fight-or-flight mode, also known as the stress response. Dr. Bessel van der Kolk is a renowned expert for his research on trauma and being the best-selling author of *The Body Keeps the Score*.

Dr. van der Kolk defines trauma as "not the story of something that happened back then, but the current imprint of that pain, horror, and fear living inside [the individual]." Traumatic events leave us stuck in a state of helplessness and terror and result in a change in how we perceive danger.

When an extremely stressful event overwhelms our nervous system, and we are unable to return to a place of feeling safe, our nervous system can change in response to the event, and we can get stuck in the stress response outside of our place of safety. We may then experience difficulty regulating emotions, being in the present moment, and engaging in fulfilling relationships.

Crisis Hotline

Early on in my healing journey, a few times, I woke up in the middle of the night feeling like I couldn't breathe. As fear gripped me, I had to sit for two hours on the edge of the bed and reassure myself I was still breathing and would be okay. The anxiety would pass, and I would lie back down and sleep. Other nights, I laid in bed for several hours before falling asleep, unsure of what was keeping me awake because I was not thinking any stressful thoughts except the thought that I wished I could go to sleep. I even thought, *What if my body has lost the ability to sleep? Can that happen?*

Then, one day, as I was exercising on my elliptical, my mind started racing, thinking, "What if anxiety overtakes me and paralyzes me to the point I cannot function and the thoughts spin up so tightly that all I want to do is escape?" I couldn't stop the thoughts as I pedaled on my elliptical that day. I call those thoughts and the feeling that came with them "the burning building feeling." At that moment, I imagined I knew a bit of the desperation a person must feel before jumping out of a burning building. I also felt I got a glimpse of what a person might feel before taking their own life.

I called the suicide/crisis prevention hotline for the first time in my life. I was not suicidal, but the intense intrusive thoughts were creating a crisis, and that was the only immediate help I could think of. It is the exact help a person should seek when they have no other immediate assistance. It was an anonymous call, and the attendant was a calming and soothing presence.

She was the first person to tell me about grounding techniques. She led me through the five senses grounding technique of looking around you and naming five things you see, four things you hear, three things you feel with your sense of touch, two things you smell, and one thing you taste. I had never heard of grounding techniques and was amazed at how the act of bringing your mind to the here and now calms your thoughts. She encouraged me to adopt it as a tool to use at any time.

I was grateful for the experience of calling the hotline and feeling the healing power of simple human connection over the telephone. I was also grateful for learning a new skill. Even though I did not consider myself suicidal, I was confident when I called that the person on the other end could help me.

If you or a loved one ever need help, in the United States, please call:

The Suicide and Crisis Lifeline at 988 or visit
988lifeline.org.

They are available by phone, chat, and text 24/7.

Outside of the United States, please search for your country's crisis and suicide hotline.

If you ever want a way out, that is a signal that a deeper thought or emotion wants to be solved. Problems, thoughts, and emotions are temporary. Even seemingly permanent problems can be solved by wrapping different thoughts around them. Don't lean out of life—lean in.

In addition to the five senses grounding technique, you can find other grounding techniques by searching online. One technique is breathing, including different patterns of breathing; there's a whole field of breathwork you can look into. Breathing is one of the quickest ways I have found to calm my mind, focus my thoughts, and center myself. I use the same technique discussed earlier in this chapter, the body scan of breathing in and out slowly while concentrating on the sensation of the breath. I only focus on the breath instead of scanning other parts of the body. You can also use words as you breathe in, such as, "I breathe in peace." As you breathe out, you could say, "I breathe out tension."

This is a long chapter, so let's take a break for a poem by the author.

When You Lean Into Life

When you lean into life,

Life leans into you.

When you press firmly in,

You find more of your truth.

When you turn up the fire

And identify true desires,

You acquire the power

To climb higher.

Stress Response

Our stress response is the way our body responds to stress. Within our window of tolerance, we feel calm and grounded. We can more freely feel joy, connection, curiosity, and empowerment. As stress increases or a traumatic event occurs, we move outside of that window of tolerance into fight or flight. If the stress persists, we move to freeze mode as a safety mechanism where we disconnect from ourselves, others, and the overwhelming feelings of fight or flight.

Window of Tolerance

Emotional Arousal/Stress Level Signs

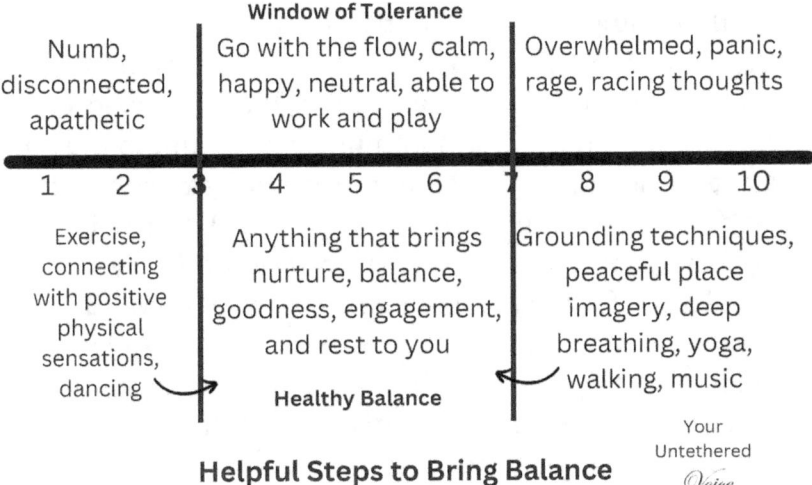

Numb, disconnected, apathetic	**Window of Tolerance** Go with the flow, calm, happy, neutral, able to work and play	Overwhelmed, panic, rage, racing thoughts
1　2	3　4　5　6	7　8　9　10
Exercise, connecting with positive physical sensations, dancing	Anything that brings nurture, balance, goodness, engagement, and rest to you **Healthy Balance**	Grounding techniques, peaceful place imagery, deep breathing, yoga, walking, music

Helpful Steps to Bring Balance

Your Untethered Voice

For reference, I have included a Window of Tolerance Diagram. The diagram demonstrates that when we define our stress level on a scale of one to ten, we want our stress to be within the range of three to seven, which is the range of healthy balance. Too little stress arousal could indicate or produce depression or apathy. Too much stress for short or long periods of time can overwhelm our mind, body, and nervous system and cause us to retreat or act out. Feeling overwhelmed can also affect our body with immediate or long-term physical symptoms. The diagram includes some helpful actions that can aid us in returning to our healthy window of tolerance or to maintain our dwelling there.

Unbeknownst to me, back in childhood my body had gotten stuck in the stress response. That stress response was not processed in a healthy way, making it even harder to process additional stressors. Then, at thirteen, I adopted the coping mechanism of disordered eating in an effort to feel safe. Believing I could control my eating made me feel I could control my body. When we believe we have control over one thing in life, it helps us feel we can control other things that currently do not feel controllable. Addiction starts when a substance or behavior numbs our pain and our mind says, "Hey, that felt good," and then returns to that same soothing agent to numb the pain again and again, thus creating an unhealthy connection. My obsessive food thoughts included wanting to eat in excess because the focus on food drowned out my pain of not feeling safe. But I knew eating in excess would cause weight gain, and I feared becoming fat. I restricted food instead of eating because that was a guarantee I would not gain excess weight. The two layers of desiring food and restricting my eating took me even further away from my painful emotions of not feeling safe. This became an addictive cycle.

A healthy nervous system can move in and out of the stress response as life stressors occur. A nervous system that has gotten stuck in fight, flight, or freeze is unable to return to feeling safe. Accessing its healthy window of tolerance becomes impaired. The good news is the nervous system can heal; we do not have to stay stuck. We can again feel safe. We feel safe by calming fear, driving it out, and healing.

Clinical cognitive neuroscientist, author, and speaker Dr. Caroline Leaf often shares a picture of the connections in our brains that continually form new pathways with every thought we think. A continual onslaught of unhealthy thoughts creates the paths for those unhealthy thoughts to continue. That continuation of harmful thoughts produces unhealthy responses in our bodies, such as the production of cortisol. Continual high levels of cortisol damage our bodies.

However, as Dr. Leaf shares, our bodies are wired for love. Not only are we wired for love, but we are wired for the good things, such as joy and peace, that bring positive biological responses within our bodies. Living in those good things is where our bodies and minds thrive.

Living in those good things also takes time, effort, and maintenance on our part because our first or primary human needs are for safety and survival. We can establish those and keep growing. If you need help anywhere along the way, please reach out to a friend, therapist, or trusted provider.

The first step to healing anything is accepting what is. This first step of acceptance is true whether we are healing ourselves or others. Through acceptance, we can calm the fight-or-flight response and begin to feel the gentle call of wholeness that beckons to us. Acceptance levels our playing field and gives us solid ground. From that space, we can make better decisions because we have calmed our minds.

The words and thoughts that heal our minds can then pour in and do their reshaping and renewing work. For our minds to be reshaped and restored, we have to take time to allow those thoughts to create new neural pathways in our brains. I first had to learn how to calm my mind and feel safe. I did that through acceptance of truth and using the calming techniques in this book. As I began to feel safe and that safety grew, healing took place.

Heal Fear

We can begin to heal fear by asking ourselves, "Why?" When we come up against resistance, fright, or fear, we can ask ourselves, "Why am I feeling this way? What am I afraid of?" When we look at our email inbox and don't want to open that email, we can ask ourselves, "What am I afraid of?" The answer may be, "I don't want to see how much I owe on that bill," or "Her husband is not doing well, and I'm afraid it will be bad news." We can acknowledge that some things are hard and some are scary, and it is okay to feel scared. We can then, with compassion, remind ourselves that we need to take the steps of courage to engage in life's responsibilities and embrace the opportunities for growth and connection.

When I learned the power of asking "Why," the revelation put more strength into my hands to heal into completion and to create wholeness. For example, "Why am I afraid of mobility decline and what can I do about it?" We need to identify the *why* of our fear to avoid missing the lesson of the fright or its cause. We can end up repeating the same predicament and engaging the same fearful response when that fear has not healed.

After reaching 110 pounds, I had difficulty going past it and maintaining a higher weight when I did go over it. I had to ask myself, "What am I afraid of?" The answer was I was afraid of not knowing the exact weight I should be. I was scared of weighing too much. I had to give myself time to work on that fear and trust myself to sense my best weight. I continued to work with my psychologist and received the coaching and support to reframe my thoughts about my weight. She explained that my weight had become strongly entrenched in my mind as my identity. I worked diligently to create a new identity. With the *why* of my fears, I could continue to heal more completely.

Weight is first about health and the point where our bodies get the nutrition they need to function at optimal levels physically and mentally. Then we want, at minimum, three to five extra pounds to cushion against times of illness or other things like stomach upset or surgery where we may experience a temporary weight loss. With a cushion in place, our bodies will not go into starvation mode to conserve energy and will continue to be able to supply our bodies with the optimum strength and energy they need to heal during those times.

To my wonder and amazement, when I got closer to 111 pounds and maintained it for a few weeks, I started experiencing even more peace emotionally as well as clarity in mental processing. I suspected that 111 pounds must be even more optimal than 110. Then, after a short time, I thought, "You know what—115 pounds is only four pounds more. Maybe I could try 115 pounds." When I heard myself say that, I knew I was graduating to a higher level in healing.

Looking Back to Look Ahead

Looking back, I realize I was perplexed about my identity and who and what I was supposed to be. The reality was I had a physical disability. Still, I rejected that label and wanted to see myself as non-disabled, but I adjusted to the limitations and was grateful to do everything I could do. When a challenge or frustration came, I kept it inside and stuffed it down, even scolding and telling myself I was not supposed to feel frustrated. I was supposed to feel victorious.

Unable to share or process my emotions because I stuffed them down into my subconscious mind, I developed a need to feel in control, so I turned to the best form of governance I could think of, which was a method of controlling my body that was possible for me...restrictive eating.

Discussion

1. Take a few moments to practice a body scan. Describe your experience and observations.

_____

_____

_____

_____

_____

2. Emotions produce physical sensations in our bodies. When you feel anger, anxiety, and compassion, where in your body do you feel them? If you cannot identify the answers right now, take note of their physical sensations the next time you feel those or other emotions.

_____

_____

_____

_____

_____

3. Journaling: Take ten minutes to write about your thoughts. Write about anything you want, whether good thoughts, thoughts of stress you want to overcome, or problems you want to solve. One method of journaling is stream of consciousness, where you write about anything that comes to your mind.

_____

_____

_____

_____

_____

4. Emotions are messengers. If you are experiencing sadness, anger, anxiety, envy, happiness, joy, or fear, list what these emotions may be signaling you to do.

_____

_____

_____

_____

Poems

Hope

Hope is your promise.
Hope is your peace.
A bastion of refuge
That transforms your release.

Out of the darkness
And into daylight,
Whether cloudy or sunny,
It is the light that grows bright.

In the glare of the sun
When the heat grows too much,
Hope is your shade
With just the right touch.

Onward you go,
With hope by your side.
Hope's always there,
Hope never hides.

Let Your Body Speak to You

Let your body speak to you,
Let it call your name.
It will tell you why you're here.
It will tell you why you came.

The joy that fills your soul,
It will guide your heart
When you open up your ears
And let it play its part.

The peace that fills your mind,
Its entrance is so grand
When you open up inside
And let it fill your land.

The breath that fills your lungs
Becomes your tool to use
To let your body speak to you
And there it shares your news.

Drink from Your Well

Drink from your well,
And let us drink, too.
Share with the world
God's image in you.

Look deep within,
Feast, and refuel.
Fill yourself up.
Take time for you.

Then flowing out
To our cups, too,
Keep pouring more,
Sharing what's true.

Wondrous rich jewels
Reside within you.
Drink from your well,
And let us drink, too.

Chapter 4
Embracing Ourselves to Heal Perfectionism and OCD

I DID NOT KNOW I HAD Obsessive-Compulsive Disorder (OCD) tendencies until my mental health therapist mentioned it. OCD is a mental illness that involves unwanted repeated thoughts and worries (obsessions) coupled with repetitive behaviors (compulsions) that a person feels they must do to address their obsessions (unwanted thoughts and worries). OCD obsessions are different from everyday unwanted thoughts. These obsessions cause a level of anxiety that affects your quality of life, and you cannot control or move past them. OCD involves the presence of obsessions and compulsions that significantly interfere with daily functioning, cause distress, and last for a significant period of time. The exact obsessions and compulsions can vary widely from person to person, and their intensity differs, too.

Any obsessive-compulsive behaviors I had recognized in my past I had labeled *perfectionism*. Obsessive-Compulsive Disorder often accompanies perfectionism. The OCD revelation made complete sense. My past struggles with obsessive food thoughts were exactly that: OCD. I linked thoughts of not feeling good enough, or feeling like I had failed, etc., to obsessive fears about weight gain, thoughts of feeling fat, overwhelming debates about whether to eat, what to eat, when to eat, whether a food was good for me, whether it had too much fat, did it have too many calories, and on and on into perfectionism. These obsessive thoughts were followed by the compulsion of restricting food or binging. The compulsion covered up and distracted me from the underlying doubts and insecurities. The act of eating or not eating became the resolution that followed the obsessive thoughts and insecurities, bringing temporary relief from them. This way of obsessing over food and food consumption became my norm, even though I knew it was not normal. I struggled to break the pattern, but when I was unsuccessful at breaking it, I ended up settling for it being "just the way I am."

The battle of the thoughts raging in my mind was sometimes intense, with one part of my mind saying, "Eat," and another part saying, "Don't eat." With all of the conflict, it became hard to decipher which voice was the wise one. I continued for years trying to solve the battle on my own until I finally got the help I needed. The knowledge that I had OCD tendencies provided a tool for me.... I could now look at other thoughts and behaviors, in areas besides food, and recognize OCD there as well.

Many of us have heard of extreme OCD cases, such as excessive hand-washing due to fear of germs, or a person developing a fear of forgetting to close their garage door when they leave their house, so every time they leave, they drive back around the block to check and ensure they closed their door. Someone may also become obsessed with order and symmetry, where objects have to be in a certain order or place, and having the objects out of order creates distress. They may engage in compulsive behaviors like counting, arranging, or aligning objects to alleviate the distress.

Let's take a closer look at some OCD behaviors so you can help yourself or someone else get the help needed to overcome OCD so it does not hinder life. First, we will look at specific eating disorder obsessions and compulsions. Then we will look at obsessions and compulsions we might hear about in a more general sense. A person with an eating disorder may also find OCD in areas outside of their eating. This book's goal is to help both those with an eating disorder and those without one to overcome areas of OCD and other mental barriers that hinder them from reaching inner wholeness.

Obsessive Thoughts with an Eating Disorder

- **Fear of Weight Gain:** Being continually preoccupied with the fear of gaining weight, even if no evidence of weight gain exists.
- **Feeling Fat:** Often feeling fat, creating obsessive and anxious thoughts about being fat, worrying about body fat composition, and even resorting to measuring body fat.
- **Body Dissatisfaction:** Persistent negative thoughts about body shape and size, leading to feelings of shame and self-disgust.
- **Food Rules:** Forming rigid rules about which foods are "allowed," "good," "bad," and "forbidden," leading to intense anxiety if these rules are broken.
- **Calorie Counting:** Obsessively calculating the caloric content of every morsel of food consumed.
- **Comparisons:** Continuously comparing one's own eating habits, body, and weight to those of others, often resulting in feelings of inadequacy or triumph.

Compulsive Behaviors of an Eating Disorder:

- **Food Restriction:** Severely limiting the quantity and variety of foods eaten, often leading to inadequate nutritional intake.
- **Compulsive Exercise:** Engaging in excessive physical activity to "burn off" calories consumed or to maintain a certain weight.
- **Binge Eating:** Consuming a large amount of food in a short period, followed by feelings of guilt and shame.
- **Purging:** Inducing vomiting, using laxatives or diuretics.
- **Food Rituals:** Cutting food into tiny pieces, eating very slowly, or arranging food in specific ways before eating.
- **Hiding Food:** Secretly storing or hoarding food, often to consume it later in private.

It's important to emphasize that these examples highlight some of the common obsessive thoughts and compulsive behaviors associated with eating disorders. The compulsion component of OCD can include both thoughts and behaviors that are designed to alleviate the mental pain of the original obsession. We can also reemphasize that if we engage in a certain conduct, it does not automatically mean we have a compulsive behavior. For example, a person could have a food ritual of eating sandwiches with a fork simply because they enjoy it. However, if they become anxious about eating a sandwich *without* a fork, the behavior has possibly become a compulsion. The key is whether the behavior hinders life and causes anxiety.

Individuals with eating disorders often experience a complex interplay of psychological, emotional, and physiological factors that contribute to their behaviors. It is a web very difficult to sort out on your own. If you or someone you know is struggling with thoughts and behaviors related to food and eating, seeking professional help from a mental health provider specializing in eating disorders is imperative for assessment, diagnosis, and appropriate treatment.

Next, let's look at other areas of obsession and compulsion, outside of eating disorders, that may hinder our lives.

Obsessions:

- **Contamination Obsessions:** Excessive fear of bacteria, germs, or dirt leading to compulsive cleaning or avoidance behaviors.

- **Fear of Harming:** Intrusive thoughts or imaginations of causing harm to oneself or others, even if one has no intention of doing so.

- **Symmetry and Order:** A strong need for things to be perfectly symmetrical or in a specific order, often resulting in compulsive arranging and aligning of objects.

- **Doubt and Uncertainty:** Persistent doubts and fears about decisions, leading to compulsive checking or seeking reassurance from others.

- **Forbidden or Taboo Thoughts:** Intruding thoughts about socially unacceptable or forbidden topics, such as violence or sexual acts.

- **Religious or Moral Obsessions:** Excessive concerns about moral or religious issues, with compulsive behaviors aimed at avoiding perceived sins or morally wrong actions. This can include fearing one has sinned even when performing ordinary or innocent behaviors and excessively performing rituals or behaviors above the prescribed number of times to ensure absolution.

Compulsions:

- **Checking:** Repeatedly checking things (like locks, appliances, or items) to prevent feared harm or danger.
- **Cleaning and Washing:** Excessive hand-washing, cleaning objects, or taking long showers to reduce contamination fears.
- **Repeating:** Engaging in repetitive actions, such as touching, tapping, or repeating words, to prevent harm or ward off distress.
- **Mental Rituals:** Performing mental acts, like counting or repeating words silently, in an attempt to neutralize obsessions.
- **Ordering and Arranging:** Arranging objects in a specific way or following rigid routines to feel a sense of control.
- **Hoarding:** Collecting and keeping items that others may perceive as useless or meaningless due to emotional attachment and fear of discarding them.

These symptoms can vary in intensity and impact from person to person. OCD is a treatable mental health condition, and a variety of therapeutic approaches and strategies can be effective in healing, reducing, or managing its symptoms. Here are some approaches:

- **Cognitive Behavioral Therapy (CBT):** This therapy aims to reduce symptoms of various mental health conditions like OCD. Especially helpful is a form called Exposure and Response Prevention (ERP).
- **Virtual Reality Exposure Therapy (VRET):** VRET uses virtual reality technology to simulate triggering situations, allowing individuals to confront and

habituate over time to their fears and obsessions in a controlled environment.

- **Mindfulness and Acceptance-Based Therapies:** These include Mindfulness-Based Stress Reduction (MBSR), Mindfulness-Based Cognitive Therapy (MBCT), and Acceptance and Commitment Therapy (ACT). They can help you develop a non-judgmental awareness of your thoughts and feelings. This awareness can help you better tolerate distressing thoughts and reduce the need to engage in compulsive behaviors. It may also allow the thoughts to dissipate.

- **Medication:** Selective Serotonin Reuptake Inhibitors (SSRIs) are commonly prescribed for OCD. They help with OCD by affecting serotonin levels in the brain. You and your doctor can determine the best treatment plan and medication duration.

- **Support Groups:** Joining a support group for individuals with OCD can provide a sense of community and understanding. Support groups provide the opportunity to share experiences and learn coping strategies from others who have similar challenges.

- **Psychoeducation:** Learning about OCD and understanding how it works can empower you to challenge your obsessions and compulsions. Education can also help you develop effective coping strategies.

Recovery from OCD is a gradual process. It's important to be patient with yourself and maintain consistency in practicing therapeutic techniques and strategies. Remember, healing from OCD may involve a combination of these approaches tailored to your specific needs and circumstances. It's essential to work closely with a mental health professional to develop a comprehensive treatment plan that addresses your unique challenges and goals.

Perfectionism

Some people are born with innate traits of thriving when things are in order. Their clothes are tidy, and they know where everything is. This is well. It becomes unwell and abnormal when those desires and traits begin to overtake their lives, and their desires for things to be a certain way become fear-based with "or else" messages and black-and-white thinking. Messages such as "I have to do this or else I won't be good enough," "If I can't get this right on the first try, then I'm not cut out for this job," "I have to wear that or look like this or else I won't receive approval." When these innate traits and drives begin interfering with our lives, and these actions and desires no longer bring joy but have crossed over into fear, clinicians classify this as clinical perfectionism.

Because I repressed emotions and did not feel the hard things, perfectionism became my moral guide and chief motivator, along with fear of other people's judgments. My core desires and motivations still existed, but they got mixed in with perfectionism. Life became confusing because some of my actions felt like me, yet other actions felt like outside forces instructing me what to do. Because of the confusion, at times, I became unsure of even which actions were mine.

While growing up, my family enjoyed having clean, shiny cars. During my childhood, Saturday afternoons included washing the car under a shade tree with a mitt and a bucket of soapy water. I enjoyed those times because I also relished seeing cars shine. However, when I got my license and my own car, perfectionism stepped in and I operated in a mix of joy and effort to obtain others' approval. The joys of a job well done got mixed in with fear of judgment and the need for self-worth.

Perfectionism combines with obsession; eventually, good is not good enough, and you are looking to make good even better, then better and better. When you run out of higher levels of better, you are left with increasing levels of anxiety because your brain has been accustomed to creating these neural pathways of better, and your body craves the chemicals these thoughts create.

Perfectionism can soon permeate everything until you believe you must be perfect at everything materially, productively, and morally. You are not perfect, so you feel like you failed, and then, in shame, you hide parts of you inside yourself. Eventually, you are hidden even from yourself. At least that is how it went for me.

As perfectionists, we're always measuring things. We're measuring whether something is good or better than before. If we are not measuring ourselves, we are measuring someone or something else. This turns into being judgmental. Many of us don't want to be judgmental, but it is true that we love others the same way we love ourselves. We cannot escape that truth.

When operating in perfectionism, we feel our actions and beliefs make us better people, superior beings. Superiority is a defense mechanism. This superiority can come in the form of feeling superior to others, as a result of comparing ourselves to others in our efforts to continually achieve higher standards. You can also perceive yourself as superior to your former self when you feel improvement over past performance makes you a better person than you were before. Better than before is good, but we want to keep it framed in joy, appreciation, and reverence, not superiority and condemnation. We must love ourselves all along the journey of personal growth. Once we learn how to make the shift in our minds from perfection- ism to excellence and balance, we learn how to hold our- selves and our thoughts in their proper space.

Not only does perfectionism make us judgmental of others, but it makes us feel our ways, thoughts, and ideas are the right ones, and that closes us off from finding better ways and ideas and from realizing there are often many good options, not just one right way. Acknowledging the truth of superiority was a hard pill to swallow. But recog- nizing the truth of it allowed me to unravel my confusion and set myself free. Because of my low self-worth, perfec- tionism did not outright make me feel superior. Instead, it made me feel isolated. I did not like having judgmen- tal thoughts because I knew being judgmental was not healthy, but I had no idea how to heal this confusing place of being judgmental, but not wanting to be. So, I retreated because the less I was around people, the less opportunity judgmental thoughts had to be triggered in my mind. Iso- lation was a place of safety where I could hide.

Letting Go of Perfectionism

The healthy alternative to perfectionism is excellence. Excellence is the pursuit of being your best through self-improvement. I emphasize *your* best. Keep ownership of it. You can be inspired, coached, and encouraged by others, but you are the one who gets to tap into, pull out, and shape the best that is within you. You get to decide what is your best.

Picture two roads running side by side; one is perfec- tionism, and one is excellence. A person can wander onto the road of perfectionism even when their intention is ex- cellence. To remain on a path of excellence and not cross over into perfectionism, we must incorporate balance. Bal- ance is a key to life: a balanced diet for a healthy body, a balanced mind for a healthy mentality, and a balanced social life for healthy relationships. Balanced sleep, a balanced work-life schedule, a balance of physical exercise, etc. Each of our life balances will look different. Your balance will be based on your needs and the balance you need to create a healthy life. And my balance will be based on my needs. The more we know ourselves, the more balance we can create in our lives.

Perfectionism is a state of trying to be in control. It seeks certainty. Perfectionists believe that by controlling our environment and outcomes, we can control our lives and circumstances.

Fear is what fuels perfectionism. The following are some of the fears a perfectionist might encounter:

- **Fear of not being good enough:** Perfectionists may have deeply-rooted feelings of inadequacy or low self-worth, leading them to believe they are only valuable when they achieve perfection.
- **Fear of losing control:** Perfectionists often seek control over their environment and outcomes as a way to reduce anxiety and uncertainty, leading them to become overly rigid and inflexible in their pursuit of perfection.
- **Fear of failure:** Perfectionists often fear making mistakes or failing to meet their or others' expectations. This fear can cause them to avoid taking risks or trying new things.
- **Fear of judgment and rejection:** Perfectionists may worry excessively about what others think of them. They fear being criticized if they don't meet perceived standards of excellence. They also fear being rejected for not meeting those high standards.
- **Fear of disappointment:** Perfectionists may fear disappointing themselves or others by not meeting

their high standards. This fear can result in relent-less self-criticism and self-imposed pressure.

- **Fear of vulnerability:** Perfectionists may avoid showing vulnerability or weaknesses because they perceive these traits as undesirable and contrary to the image they strive to maintain.
- **Fear of making the wrong choice:** Perfectionists can struggle with decision-making, fearing that any choice will be flawed or have negative consequences.
- **Fear of not being loved or accepted for who they are:** Perfectionists may associate their self-worth with their achievements and believe that being perfect is the only way to be loved or accepted by others.

Perfectionism is a relentless critic. It can permeate a person's whole life. Perfectionism permeates an eating disorder. It adds more fuel to the desire to be in control of your body. By controlling your body, you feel you can control your emotions. In reality, you are burying your emotions and covering them up with this feeling of control. Control becomes the distraction that keeps your emotions buried. If the feelings start rising to the surface, you exert more control to push them back down. Perfectionism produces more and more control. You try harder to control what you already control; when that is not enough, you find more things to control. Perfectionism not only works like that with an eating disorder, but it works like that with all addictions and situations.

When a person has perfectionism in one area, it often doesn't just stay in one area. It flows through all areas of life like threads flow through a garment. Perfectionists can be high achievers, driven to succeed, and they can also be afraid to try things, paralyzed by a fear of failure, fearing it won't work, so they just don't try. A part of them may want to try, but they don't attempt to because their fear is too great.

I was a high achiever in high school with a successful goal of getting good grades. However, I avoided some classes I felt would be too challenging, like geometry. Math was a weaker area, and geometry, with all of the shapes and angles, I believed would be too hard for my mind to comprehend. I later identified this challenge with shapes and angles as a deficit in spatial perception.

After high school, I struggled to find my place in life. I was limited by my disability, reserved and withdrawn within, not confident of my strengths, not knowing the power of connection and support, and taking for granted that we grow over time in knowledge and wisdom instead of obtaining it all at once. As a perfectionist, I felt I was supposed to have it all together and be instantly strong, wise, and knowledgeable. I didn't have it all together and wasn't instantly strong, wise, and knowledgeable. I did not have all the answers, so I hid inside myself.

I tried to go to college with the financial aid of our state's vocational rehabilitation program, but the pursuit of college classes was overwhelming. I also feared the pursuit of higher education might alter my religious belief system.

I was still unaccepting of my disability. I felt the disability made me less than the perfect person I was trying to be. Our culture still looked at a disability as a flaw, and I believed the lie. Disabilities are not flaws; they are differences. They are differences that allow the gifts of acceptance and creativity to step up to the plate and engage with life.

While growing up in my parents' home and having only a few necessary accommodations in school like extra time to finish tests, extra time to get to classes, and a few minutes early dismissal to get to the bus after school, I was still able to brush the reality of disability into a corner and try to close the door. My mobility was good enough not to need special accommodations in the home, and the only thing I needed outside of the home was a railing when using stairs. Walking on uneven ground was challenging, but I managed it when necessary.

Therefore, my personal unfamiliarity with disability and this new concept of needing to navigate the realities of it as I entered adult life created a storm inside. Perfectionism, the eating disorder, and every other insecurity I held created a very hard storm to escape because my eating disorder was a distraction from the turmoil. It enabled me to keep the tempest buried. And the storm inside raged.

I felt my way past my shame and disappointment of not attending college and continued with life. When I was twenty-three, I attended a Bible college in Ohio for one year. After that, I continued to be active in my church, prayed, and studied my Bible, had my own apartment, and enjoyed all the activities of maintaining a home. I wanted my relationship with God, my time in prayer and Bible study, and my participation in my church to bring healing to the ache inside that I still carried. It was an ache I knew was there, but I could not access it. The eating disorder stood in the way.

I even thought, *What if God is waiting on me? What if I'm not doing something he wants me to do?* I had remotely wondered if counseling would help. By that time, I was more accepting of the validity of counseling, but I was unsure how to determine whom to go to. I also rejected the idea of counseling because I wanted a quick fix, as in one or two appointments, and the eating disorder was gone. I had too many other things I wanted to do so I reasoned I did not have long durations of time to spend addressing an eating disorder. I could not picture how one or two appointments could heal the eating disorder, so I did not go to counseling.

I wanted God to take responsibility for healing my eating disorder. I wanted him to do all of the work. I wanted my relationship with him to be the key to unlock the door, but the key to unlock the door was my relationship with me. My relationship with myself is where the key was stored.

I've learned to look deep inside. The eating disorder kept me out of the inside. The pattern of eating mainly at night was an avenue of comfort as well as a means to accomplish tasks without distraction. I was able to anticipate the food and allow that anticipation to provide a distraction from the anxiety inside, even though I did not know the true identity of the pain.

In the midst of healing the eating disorder, I also found healing for perfectionism. We can take steps to heal perfectionism. We can begin to practice embracing imperfection. We can learn to cultivate self-compassion. We can heal self-confidence. And we can heal self-worth. These are steps that have worked for me, and I want to share them with you now in more detail.

Embrace Imperfection

Taking the small step of retraining our minds will allow us to begin to walk the road of healing perfectionism. We can start with the smallness of embracing a tiny imperfection and building to big. I began by allowing things like the spices on my spice rack to become out of order. I observed that the earth did not quake, nor did I obsess about the spices; I was able to go about my day not even thinking about them. Then, I began to practice allowing things others did or did not do to be laid to rest instead of picking the thoughts up and being anxious about them.

From there, I added allowing my actions to be imperfect. If I stumbled over a word while speaking or pronounced a syllable incorrectly, I realized the listener did not judge me, nor did I become a person of less intelligence in my own mind. I began to let myself be human and embrace the joys of life. That's what letting go of perfectionism can do for you.

Next, I also realized and developed acceptance that my less-than-perfect housekeeping is not a pinnacle upon which I am judged. The purpose of our home is to serve us with shelter, peace, joy, and comfort. That is enough if our home safely serves us and allows our souls to prosper. We can always adjust, change, or rearrange physical things or levels of care in our homes to suit our needs or change the atmosphere to bring inspiration. If our home is safe and serving us, and someone chooses to judge us, that is something for them to deal with. Their judgments and opinions do not have to affect us.

Practice Self-Compassion

In 2021, when my cousin became ill with a brain tumor, his wife posted a picture on social media of a book her friend had given her to read in the midst of this trying time. She talked of the powerful impact *When Things Fall Apart* by Pema Chödrön had on her. I decided to read the book since it had been so powerful in a trying time like hers. I listened to an audio copy, and I was immediately drawn into the depths of its truths. The biggest gift I came away with from that book was the gift of self-compassion.

The book taught me how to sit with myself through the hard times. Whether it's a challenging period in life, a hard day, a hard moment, a hard thought, or a hard memory, sit with yourself, have compassion, and don't run. Compassion will say, "Yes, this is hard; yes, it's okay to feel sad, grief, lonely, or whatever hard feelings you are feeling." Compassion will then give self a hug, and self will have the strength to take the next step, the next, and the next into a place of healing.

Heal Self-Confidence

It is important to heal self-confidence when healing perfectionism. Self-confidence is closely related to the external factors of performance and achievement. From my perspective, my life had consisted of some accomplishments and a greater number of failures. I had accomplished having an apartment, but I had not accomplished having a career.

I had tried to move into the arena of gainful employment to support myself, but I was out of touch with the realities of my disability and the capacity of what my body and my own psyche could handle. Plus, my low self-confidence always told me that someone else could do the job better than I could. In my mind, I was supposed to do everything a neurotypical person could do who had no limitations. After all, we are all supposed to be able to do anything we set our minds to, right? Marrying reality and those ideas was confusing because I was unaware of how to join them together with compassion and truth. At age twenty-five, I applied and was approved for Disability by the government.

I participated in volunteer opportunities, but even in those, I felt like I had failed because when I would cease from any of them, it was usually because I felt overwhelmed, whether or not the volunteer duty caused the sense of being overwhelmed. At that time, I had not yet developed the knowledge and skills to evaluate my emotions as true and valid, so I felt defeated instead.

Self-confidence is a belief in our abilities, skills, and judgments and a feeling of being capable and competent. One day, I discovered a person I had met with several times through virtual project meetings had cerebral palsy with some similar physical challenges to mine. I respected and admired this lady and her career in social services. She was widowed when her children were young, and she went to college after her husband's death and obtained a Master of Social Work. As we talked about her experience, I found myself apologizing for not obtaining a college degree. She stopped there and said, "Tracy, no one knows what you've been through like you do." She continued on with additional affirming words, but I do not remember the rest of what she shared because my heart had melted at the point of her first words, and I felt the compassion pouring in. People could have said things like that to me before, but the right words spoken at the right time when we can wrap our minds around their meaning can have an even more profound impact.

As I have continued to grow my belief in my abilities, skills, and judgments and have matured my perception that I am capable and competent, I've grown in peace. I've found we must gently observe and identify our own abilities and skills. We must build trust in our own judgments by embracing the values and morals that we hold as true. We must then live according to those values and morals in the midst of people who hold the same and differing values, always willing to be polished by the knowledge and views of others. That willingness to be polished by the values and views of others is meekness or humility. We can bump up against differing views, respect them, and decide whether or not their views might have some truths we want to consider making our own. After making our decision, we can then realize we can also co-exist with differing views.

When we are sure and confident of our values, views, and judgments, we have the bold strength to stand in who we are and to allow other ideas to pass through the land of our lives. Some ideas will pass right on through, and some will leave a fragrance, an aroma, or a structural change.

Heal Self-Worth

Self-worth comes from internal factors such as identity and belongingness and is related to a person's sense of personal value and self-respect. It refers to the inherent value and worth you give yourself regardless of external elements such as success or failure.

Due to the intrinsic value of every living being, a value birthed at the beginning of creation, we are all of beautiful and magnificent worth. We carry unique traits, strengths, and weaknesses that make each of us a wonder to be explored and shared with the world. We build on our strengths and use creativity to shore up our weaknesses.

Self-worth is built over time. Little by little in my healing journey, I had been peeling away the layers of shame and feeding self-worth, coming to believe more and more that I have valuable gifts to offer the world, not only believing it with my head but feeling the ground of it growing solid beneath my feet. Self-worth is not only something we build inside; it is grown and nurtured through relationships. I had been discovering and gathering a growing community of people who also believe all humans have great things to give the world if they only believe, reach down deep inside, and have the courage to say "yes."

Abundance

When we know the fullness of our self-worth and build our self-confidence, we can create a path into the fullness of life. When we say "yes," we can enter into the arena of the universe's abundance. The idea of abundance can get a bad name because it is often associated with financial abundance. However, it is more than financial abundance. It is abundance in relationships, abundance in thoughts, and abundance in opportunities. It is swinging your arms wide open and making room for everyone to thrive to their utmost. It is having no competition or jealousy when someone meets their highest goals; instead, it's knowing when we each reach our goals, we all prosper. It is believing we can all continue to climb higher in personal development for our entire lives. As we all develop ourselves, share our knowledge and discoveries with others, and thrive to our highest potential, the world evolves into a better place.

As I was meditating on this thought of abundance and doing some research for this book, I began having a "what if?" thought about reaching people with the message in this book. The thought remained in my mind and got bigger. Then I stepped back and thought, *Hey, this feels good, and it's different than in the past.* In the past, I would have been minimizing myself and the opportunity and even berating myself for thinking such grand thoughts, for dreaming such beautiful dreams. All of a sudden, a feeling filled my chest and flooded my heart, and the words came to mind, "I am worthy!" I am worthy to dream those dreams. I am worthy to accomplish those goals. I am worthy to do the things that are in my heart.

And you are worthy, too. What it takes for each of us to experience abundance and accomplish goals is to build the needed skills, gather the tools or support, create community, and have the courage to say, "Yes!" We all have the same worth and value. Whether you are the richest person in the world or the poorest, whether you possess the highest IQ or not, we are all equal in worth. Knowing you have worth can unlock doors and give you the boldness and confidence to step through.

Discussion

1. Do you recognize symptoms of OCD in yourself? What steps can you take to begin to address and heal the OCD?

_____

_____

_____

_____

2. Do you feel you need to let go of perfectionism? If so, what thoughts, emotions, and behaviors make you feel this way?

_____

_____

_____

_____

3. From the list of fears that fuel perfectionism, write down any that stood out for you, including why they stood out.

_____

_____

_____

_____

4. Do you love (cherish and nurture) yourself where you are now and where you were in the past? If you love yourself now, but didn't in the past, what brought about the change?

_____

_____

_____

_____

5. If you need to begin loving yourself, what can you do to start that journey?

_____

_____

_____

_____

6. Do you have any mental or emotional struggles you've put off addressing because you felt you did not have time to tend to them? If so, what are they? Do you plan to address them now, and what step will you take next to begin to work on them?

_____

_____

_____

_____

7. What imperfections of your own can you embrace by accepting them, and how will you embrace them?

_____

_____

_____

_____

8. What situations in your own life are in need of your self-compassion right now?

_____

_____

_____

_____

9. On a scale of one to ten, how strong is your self-confidence?

---

10. Name three treasures of worth, strengths, or traits you have inside.

---

11. Meditate on the truth, calmness, and reassurance of this scripture: "For God has not given us a spirit of fear, but one of power, love, and sound judgment" (2 Timothy 1:7, CSB). Write down any insights that come to you.

Poems

Untangle the Threads

Untangle the threads
Of your patched-up life,
And thread the needle
To sew the new tapestry
Of brilliant colors
And clever design.

Enough

Grasping *enough,*
The completion of your being.
The beauties and the wonders,
The seen and unseen things.

The gains and the losses
That made you who you are.
The wisdom that's within you,
You are a shining star.

You stand there today
Right there where you are.
You are *enough*,
You've come so very far.

You will grow, you will stretch,
You will cry, you will rest.
You will abide in your all
Because you are your best.

Right there where you are,
In the smooth or the rough,
Stand up straight and tall
Because you are *enough*.

Chapter 5
Expanding Spirituality

A S CHRISTIANS, WE ARE OFTEN told the Bible has all of the answers, but God is so much bigger than that, and he did not intend for the Bible to be a stand-alone book. The Bible holds the foundation of the Christian faith, and it contains an abundance of our great and precious promises, but life is so much more, and God is so much more. Life is about living from the goodness of your inner being and having connections with others. We were created for the purpose of having connection with him and connection with others.

My Church History

I grew up in a Protestant denomination that believed the Bible was the only book you needed to know in order to live a good, balanced, moral life. "The Bible has all of your answers" was a common belief. My opinion now is that people within different denominations will believe that the Bible has all of their answers in various degrees, differing from person to person. In the past, with my black-and-white thinking and literal view of everything, I believed I needed to rely on God alone to give me all my answers to anything mental, emotional, or thought-related. Mental and emotional struggles, pains, and disappointments were supposed to be solved only through my communion with God.

That method works for none of us. We all need connections with other people to help us maintain good mental health. Good relationships with others keep us mentally healthy simply through sharing conversations and giving and receiving in the midst of them. The conversations allow us to receive and process thoughts and physiologically create new connections in our brains, allowing our minds to grow and restructure unhealthy pathways into healthy paths. Furthermore, when we encounter thoughts, hardships, and deeply painful situations, reaching out when needed to professionals, who are trained and skilled in helping us process those thoughts, can be vital for proceeding with a healthy life.

Law of Attraction

One day early in my healing journey, I was watching a tagline of video streaming as I walked on my elliptical machine. It was playing videos about religion and spirituality. Footage started playing about the Law of Attraction. I thought, "Whoa, this is out there, past what I've watched before," but I continued to watch with curiosity. The speaker started to talk about us asking the power of the Universe to bring things to us. I was thinking at that moment, *Uh, maybe I shouldn't be watching this.* Then, in the same fashion that a dimmed light gets brighter, I saw the thought turn on, *Wait, I know The Power of the Universe. It's God!* Then, I scrambled to find whether the speaker believed in God. It seemed she did, though her exact beliefs about God as our source, I do not know. But what mattered is the video opened my eyes to a new revelation of God as being even bigger than I had imagined before. Prior to that, I saw him as up in heaven, sending his answers from there in a narrow pathway straight down from above. But since that moment, I see him as God inhabiting the universe and sending his answers from many directions throughout the whole expanse of the infinite cosmos. Now, when I pray, I often ask God to send the powers of his universe to work on behalf of whatever I am praying about. The first time I prayed like that, I was amazed at how much that prayer increased my faith. Praying and imagining God's power coming from all directions to work on my behalf brings a robust feeling to my faith. No more are my prayers a two-way narrow avenue between God and me; now, when I pray, I speak my prayer in the midst of the vastness of the universe. I see a God who has the liberty to summon his forces from all directions on my behalf.

This was significant because I grew up with Protestant Christian beliefs that promoted the idea that we should not give thought to other spiritual or religious beliefs outside our denomination. That fear kept me penned up in my own inner barnyard to the point of not being able to listen to other ministers, read other Christian books, or learn about other religions for fear of my mind straying and getting off of what we believed was the straight and narrow way to Heaven. The spirit of fear we thought God set us free from was taking rule in our lives without us knowing it. We also focused so much on going to heaven that we forgot God first put us here on earth to take our place, share the gifts and beauty inside of us, play our part in the universe as he moves the world forward, enjoy life, and grow with him. He wants to delight in us, his creation, as we grow, blossom, and bloom.

The degree of exclusive belief each person holds collaborates with each individual's own thoughts and personality to direct them. Thereby, some people walk deeper into exclusion beliefs than others; when too exclusive, they can miss out on the true liberty for which we were created, which is joy, peace, and unity with God and all of humankind.

The only view I can describe is the one from the place where I stood and the beliefs I held. For me, my place was one of great devotion to God and of great fear of straying. I did not know this fear hindered me; I thought it kept me safe.

From then until my early forties, I remained a Christian who believed we should only learn of Christian beliefs and should reject exploring or accepting anything from any other belief system. This included, for example, the belief to stay away from yoga because yoga teaches dangerous religious practices. The truth about yoga is the physical movements of the practice are very beneficial for the body, and you can worship whatever god you choose to worship or think whatever thoughts you choose to think while moving your body in yoga routines.

We also gain many benefits from learning about meditation, studying the Buddhist act of emptying ourselves, soaking up the devotion of the monks, and feasting at the tables of the Muslims while exploring the things we don't know. My hope is for people to set themselves free from the fear of other religions to explore other beliefs. In John 10, Jesus describes how his sheep hear his voice, and another they will not follow. We benefit from developing enough trust in ourselves and trust in God to believe he will direct us as we explore his vast world and its many religions and spiritual practices. We can begin by setting people free to live in liberty and be the person they were created to be within this vast universe. I can guarantee you there is a thought or piece of information out there that you have not heard before that will enrich your life. I look forward to delving deeper into the study of other religious beliefs and spiritual practices.

While exploring, we do not have to accept every principle of a religion or practice. Still, we enrich ourselves when we become open and curious about what our Creator may say to us as we explore. We can incorporate the ideas we believe are true and say no to the ideas we do not believe in, or we can let them lie on the ground of the universe and allow the openness in our minds to know we may, in the future, grasp other aspects of them we do not understand now.

Meditation and Mindfulness

In my late thirties or early forties, when I became interested in essential oils, I began to reflect on how in biblical times, essential oils were widely used and incorporated into life because natural remedies were the only medicines in existence. They were a welcome part of life and were known in the ancients' cultures.

I realized that, in a similar way, people in biblical times were familiar with meditation. The events in the Bible took place in Middle-Eastern society, where they would have been familiar with meditation and other spiritual practices. In my mid-forties, I began to hear about meditation as a tool for good mental health. In my Christian community, we were cautious of these practices and the way they may open our minds to other religions or thoughts. Therefore, I was reluctant to try meditation. As I encountered more sources discussing meditation benefits, I thought about the Bible's discussion of meditation and realized the people back then were already familiar with meditation through cultural exposure. Often in the Bible, meditation refers to *thinking and pondering*. We often receive a brief mention of thoughts and ideas in the Bible, but the people back then lived with the whole cultural experience and had a depth of knowledge not fully conveyed to us in the Bible's brief pages.

Various forms of meditation exist, and the act of meditation does not have to be about religion. Meditation does provide a beautiful way to incorporate thoughts about your religion, any religion, into your mind. Still, mindful meditation, the kind often encouraged for mental health, is, foremost, the act of calming your mind and strengthening your ability to direct your thoughts.

"Mindfulness is the aware, balanced acceptance of the present experience. It isn't more complicated than that. It is opening to or receiving the present moment, pleasant or unpleasant, just as it is, without either clinging to it or rejecting it."

— Sylvia Boorstein

Meditation helps you begin to learn how to calm your thoughts. It is similar to physical exercise in that the more you practice it, the stronger you grow. As I began to practice meditation, my thoughts began to calm. From a space of awe and wonder, I began to observe times I had peace when, before, I would have had anxiety. Times I was calm when, before, thoughts of anger would have come rushing in. At times when something happened and fear rose up, I was able to pause and calm that fear with compassion. The more you meditate, the better you can live authentically, thoroughly, and as the you whom you were created to be.

At first, when I began to meditate, I was filled with doubt that I would be able to calm my mind and focus my thoughts. Doubt will be your biggest foe and the first enemy you will engage. However, you don't engage it with force; you engage it with peace and belief. You conquer it with persistence and determination.

One of the easiest methods of mindful meditation is a meditation focusing on the breath. Right now where you are, take a slow, deep breath in through your nose and exhale through your mouth. Repeat the same process while focusing on the sensation of the air coming in through your nose, and let it out. Then, repeat it again, focusing on where you feel the sensation most in your torso. As you breathe in, do you feel it mostly in your chest? In your abdomen?

Slow, deep breaths also activate our vagus nerve. The vagus nerve is one of the longest nerves in the body and runs from the brainstem down into the abdomen. It affects several organs, including the heart, lungs, stomach, and intestines. It plays an important role in the parasympathetic nervous system in regulating the involuntary body functions of digestion, heart rate, and breathing.

Another mindful meditation form is guided meditation. You can find numerous apps and videos online with guided meditations. If, like I was, you are fearful of meditation and any unwelcome ideas it might bring, remember you are in control. You choose what guided meditations to listen to. If you are uncomfortable with one, you can stop playing it and find another. Meditation's goal is to help you focus your mind into a place of peace.

An additional simple mindful meditation technique is eating mindfully. The next time you eat, focus on the flavor of each bite. Savor that flavor and describe it. Then, focus on the texture of the food. Is it creamy? Is it crunchy? Try concentrating on the sensation of your food as it goes down your throat. You can also engage in the practice of chewing each bite of food a set number of times as a way to eat mindfully.

In addition to the psychological benefits of mindful eating, our physiology benefits, too. Mindful eating triggers a calming of the parasympathetic nervous system. This response is also known as the "rest and digest" response. When we are in a state of relaxation, such as during mindful eating, the response stimulates the release of digestive juices such as saliva, stomach acid, and pancreatic enzymes that help break down food and increase nutrient absorption.

Meditation can become a lifelong practice and a place of growth. It will become a practice you can access anytime and anywhere. It is a powerful way to engage more deeply with your Creator, religion, spiritual practice, and yourself. The only ingredient you need to meditate is you.

Four Key Inspiring Books

During my healing journey, a special period of time occurred when I read key books that really spoke to me and brought healing and growth. One of them was Jill Bolte Taylor's *My Stroke of Insight: A Brain Scientist's Personal Journey*. Taylor was a brain scientist at Harvard when she had a stroke. She recounts, in fascinating detail, what it was like to experience the stroke and her long journey of recovery. The brain has always fascinated me, but her book opened up a greater understanding of how the different parts of the brain each do their own job yet flow and coordinate together. Her stroke occurred on the left side of her brain, so that side ceased functioning for a time. Her experience opened my eyes to a greater understanding of spirituality and gave me a deeper reverence for my own brain injury and the marvels of which parts worked and which were damaged, the rerouting that occurred, and the deficits that remain.

Through her experience and scientific knowledge, Taylor received insight into the brain's Four Characters and developed the Four Characters brain model, which she shares in detail in her second book, *Whole Brain Living: The Anatomy of Choice and the Four Characters That Drive Our Life*. Her second book was another of the four books that brought me great insight and healing.

The Four Characters gave me an understanding of my own various characters and the gifts they bring. For example:

- **Character One—Organizer Me:** This character brings gifts but can also be overpowering. Its strengths can be neglected or underappreciated when we are overwhelmed.
- **Character Two—Tender Me:** I fell in love with this character. It is the place of our deep emotional needs and griefs, the part of us that sometimes needs a hug, a good cry, or some comforting encouraging words to empower us to stand back up and join back in.
- **Character Three—Joyful, Carefree Me:** I came to cherish this character. It taught me how a little fun is good for all of us.
- **Character Four—Spiritual Me:** I am in awe of this character's gift. It connects me with my Creator and administers compassion to the tender me when she needs nurturing or tender loving care.

The next book that inspired me was *Sitting at the Feet of Rabbi Jesus* by Lois Tverberg. When someone told me they were in a group study of that book and described it, I was intrigued to read it. I wanted to know more about the culture in which Jesus had lived.

I learned rabbis, in that time, were teachers who traveled from place to place instructing the people. They selected disciples to serve their needs and the needs of their work. They attracted followers who wanted to hear what they had to say. Jesus was one rabbi and teacher, among many others in Israel. He was indeed considered a great teacher in those days, but to most of the Jews, he was just a teacher, not the prophesied Messiah.

I learned the Jewish culture was one of community or a collective culture, in contrast to our modern Western culture, which is a culture of individualism. I learned how God values community, connection, and relationships. As well as valuing the individual, he values what is good for the whole. The passage in the Bible (quoted below) about the Body of Christ being a whole made up of parts, with each part doing its work, came alive even more in my mind. I gained a greater understanding of the beauty of God's love, his cherishing affection toward humanity, and how we are each a part of the Body that is creating and carrying out the function of the whole.

1 Corinthians 12:12-27, NIV

Just as a body, though one, has many parts, but all its many parts form one body, so it is with Christ. For we were all baptized by one Spirit so as to form one body—whether Jews or Gentiles, slave or free—and we were all given the one Spirit to drink. Even so the body is not made up of one part but of many.

Now if the foot should say, "Because I am not a hand, I do not belong to the body," it would not for that reason stop being part of the body. And if the ear should say, "Because I am not an eye, I do not belong to the body," it would not for that reason stop being part of the body. If the whole body were an eye, where would the sense of hearing be? If the whole body were an ear, where would the sense of smell be? But in fact God has placed the parts in the body, every one of them, just as he wanted them to be. If they were all one part, where would the body be? As it is, there are many parts, but one body.

The eye cannot say to the hand, "I don't need you!" And the head cannot say to the feet, "I don't need you!" On the contrary, those parts of the body that seem to be weaker are indispensable, and the parts that we think are less honorable we treat with special honor. And the parts that are unpresentable are treated with special modesty, while our presentable parts need no special treatment. But God has put the body together, giving greater honor to the parts that lacked it, so that there should be no division in the body, but that its parts should have equal concern for each other. If one part suffers, every part suffers with it; if one part is honored, every part rejoices with it.

Now you are the body of Christ, and each one of you is a part of it.

I learned Hebrew thinking is based on action and experience, contrasted to Western society's thinking being based on logic, which we inherited from the Greeks. We Westerners try to figure everything out with logic, whereas the Hebrews wanted to walk in truth and live in truth; it is an experience and an encounter. Hebrew thought is experiential and believes we cannot define or comprehend God. Western culture wants to define truth and define God rather than first trusting that in him we live, move, and have our being. Hebrews want to do good and want to know how to do that; Westerners want to be good and define how to be that.

At the same time I was reading *Sitting at the Feet of Rabbi Jesus*, I was also reading *When Things Fall Apart*, the book my cousin's wife read at the beginning of my cousin's battle with cancer as I mentioned in the last chapter. It struck me that even though the two books were based on two different religions, their messages complemented one another.

This thought furthered my meditation on the ability to receive good things from other religions without being required to embrace the whole belief system, if I so choose. While growing up, we had a saying among our church members, "Don't throw the baby out with the bathwater." In other words, "Don't dispose of all the thoughts just because you are disposing of a few." We applied it when the preacher said something we disagreed with. But I was now learning I could apply it in studying other religions. I did not have to fear learning about other religions the way my church had led me to believe. I can bask in the truths of those religions, too, just like I can bask in the truths of the religion I grew up with. A good memoir about Christians exploring other religions is Barbara Brown Taylor's *Holy Envy*.

Discussion

1. Are there any religions or spiritual practices you are curious to study?

_____

_____

_____

_____

2. Are you interested in reading any of the books mentioned in this chapter? If so, which ones?

_____

_____

_____

_____

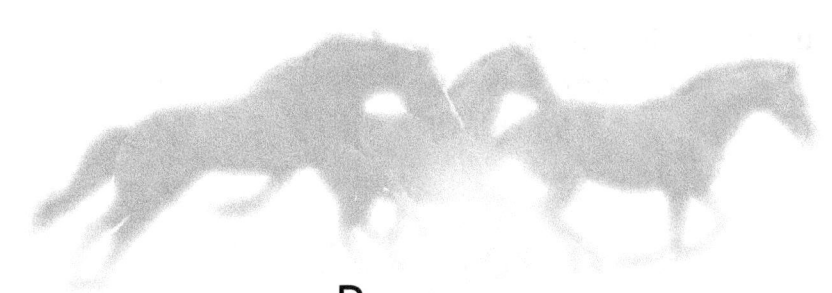

Poems

Our Fears

We are limited by
The truths we don't know
While living the
Truths we hold dear.

We cast aside so
Many stakes in our lives
While running
Away from our fears.

When we turn and look
Our fears in the face,
We oft' may truly find
Their power is erased.

When You Get in Touch with God

When you get in touch with God,
You get in touch with you.
When you grasp what's in your heart,
You grasp your deepest truths.

If your joy is radiant
Or if your heart is blue,
When you get in touch with God,
You get in touch with you.

Deeper into God brings you
Deeper into you.
You accept this in your heart
And find your deepest truths.

If you have not heard this,
If it's new to you,
Our Creator is in awe,
And he's deeply into you.

At the center of your being,
You will find our Highest King.
He is right there waiting
To introduce you to you.

Together, you co-create.
You open up the gates
Of the goodness and the truth
Deep within you.

When you get in touch with you,
You get in touch with God.
You have found the luscious clay,
You have found the luscious sod.

Chapter 6
Waking Up to Dreams

A LMOST IMMEDIATELY AFTER I STARTED working with my mental health therapist who specializes in eating disorders, I began having dreams. These dreams had a recurring theme and continued for a year and a half. Dreams are a fascinating phenomenon because they speak to us. They carry a message to us from our minds and spirits. They are our mind's way of sorting our thoughts and collaborating with our intuition.

The night before my second session with my therapist, I dreamed I needed to get to school. I was driving in my car and caught up with a bus transporting students on a field trip. I went into the building the students went into, which turned out to be a busy shopping mall with tables outside the stores. I had an urgent feeling that I needed to get back to my car, but I didn't know how to find it. I was browsing items and came upon a vendor selling books; it was an exciting distraction that deterred me for a few minutes. Then I remembered I still needed to find my car. I walked on and found a lady who said she would help me find my automobile. We walked through the milling crowd and approached a set of automatic sliding doors. The doors opened and I stepped through, expecting the lady to accompany me. But when I turned around, she was gone. I felt fearful at first, but I kept walking and found my car.

I'm blessed with a therapist who gets excited about dreams, too, because of the power they hold for the human mind and spirit. As I relayed this dream to her, she thought this dream could be talking about counseling because the office she was in had a set of bookcases behind her filled with books. The woman in the dream was indeed possibly my therapist, and once I went with her, I was able to get back on the right path and find my car. As I relive the dream, I also marvel at how fascinating it was when I turned around and she was gone because, even then, I thought, "Wow, this is like something you see in books or movies!" Looking back now, I can also wonder if the books in the mall had a dual meaning and were pointing to me writing a book. But that is the fun thing about dreams; we can hold them up to the light, look at their various possibilities, and not have to lock ourselves into one interpretation.

After that first dream, I started having dreams that contained a specific common thread, even though each dream was never exactly alike. I was always in school, trying to find my classes and remember my class schedule. I was never sure what classes I had, what order they were in, or where to find the classrooms, but I was somehow in the background or off-camera, still getting to my classes, completing the assignments, and proceeding through the school year. A few times in my dreams, I thought how helpful it would be if I had a copy of my class schedule; then, I could feel confident and reassured of what classes I had, where, and when instead of just hoping I made it to my classes and through the school year.

When we have a recurring dream, we should take note because it means our minds are pondering a message.

These dreams continued for a year and a half, not every day, but, on average, about every two weeks—just enough to keep my spark of intrigue well-lit. The dreams added extra fascination to my journey.

One dream I especially remember started with me in a school lobby outside of the main building. I was not feeling well, and I was trying to decide if I should go into the school or go home. A school administrator was there, but at that moment, he was in the lobby changing a light bulb. This man, in my real life, had been one of my school bus drivers during childhood. He was someone I respected and thought highly of.

I told him I was pondering whether to go home since I did not feel well. Talking it out with him helped me decide going home would be best. He then told me the school had an electric wheelchair I could use to get back to my car. I was stunned because I'd had no idea the school had an electric wheelchair on hand. It was remarkable they had that available. I got into the wheelchair and went part of the way to my car. Then I came upon a fair of vendors and got out of the wheelchair to walk on the short winding path through their setup. I scanned over some tables with books as I walked by. At the end of the path was a fellow browser whom I greeted with a hello. In my real life, she was a fellow congregant at my childhood church, and she is a dear family friend today. I continued walking and reached my car at the dream's end.

Most of the dreams seemed to be in a high school setting. Sometimes, the building had similarities to my real high school, and sometimes not. A couple of the dreams were elementary school settings, with the building bearing a lot of resemblance to my elementary school. However, I was not necessarily elementary-age because, in one of my dreams, I was trying to remember where I parked my car.

During the period I had these recurring dreams, I was working with my therapist on mental health and my registered dietitian on weight gain and a healthy relationship with food; I was coming to know food as fuel and friend instead of my enemy. I also went to a physical medicine doctor to gain direction about my legs and mobility.

My mobility was slowly deteriorating, so I was trying to gain direction for going forward. At first, it seemed my right knee was a key problem and was hyper-extending. Both the doctor and physical therapist could see a slight hyperextension, but not a large amount. The physical therapy did not work for me, so I explored a leg brace. The brace was my request, though the doctor advised me that sometimes braces do not work out. But I wanted to try it because I would not know for myself until I tried. The leg brace was awkward. It did make my right leg feel secure and stable, but it created an imbalance in my pelvis and left leg; one reason was the brace was only on one leg, and it was also so bulky and heavy. The brace was also purposely snugly molded to the patient's leg.

I was on a weight-gain journey and knew the brace might need adjustments or replacement in the future because of size changes, but I chose to keep that in the back of my mind instead of acknowledging it could be a drawback. Foremost, because of the awkwardness of the brace, I began to understand why the first preference is to strengthen the body or find ways to function without a brace because braces can be cumbersome, and many patients give up on them, which is exactly what I did. Truthfully, I was relieved the weighty brace did not work out for me; that oddly gave me a sense of freedom.

The leg brace had brought to my attention that my left leg felt unstable at the hip. I realized I had sensed it but had not recognized it because I was so focused on what I thought was hyperextension of my right knee. When I walked or exercised on my stepper, my leg felt like it was slightly twisting at the hip.

When I expressed concern to my physical medicine doctor, he watched me walk and said he saw a sway in my pelvis that indicated muscle weakness. So, he ordered physical therapy. He had noted at previous appointments that my neck was tight, so we decided to have the therapist give me advice and exercises for the neck tightness as well.

During this time, I also had some facial pressure that had been going on for several months. The pressure was triggered when I sat, especially at my desk; a few times the pain reached a nine on a scale of one to ten. When the pressure got that bad, I wondered if I should go to the emergency room, but I knew from experience that the pressure subsided when I lay down overnight in bed. So, instead of going to the ER, I would lie down, hoping I was making the right decision and trusting I'd feel better in the morning, which I did.

I had talked to my primary care doctor's nurse when the pressure first started occurring, and she had recommended trying Flonase for allergies because that would be the doctor's first recommendation. When I tried it, it seemed to reduce the pressure a notch, so I thought maybe we had found that allergies were the cause. I also wondered about sinus conditions, though I had no sinus congestion or runny nose.

I also talked with my physical medicine doctor several times about this face pressure since I was seeing him regularly. We discussed the possibility of it being sinus-related, and I shared with him that it seemed to be triggered by sitting. He mentioned seeing an ENT as a future consideration. I was hoping he would refer me to an ENT then. He didn't, so I made an appointment myself.

The ENT appointment occurred right after the physical therapy visits ended. I continued doing the exercises for my neck and shoulders. The ear, nose, and throat doctor decided to prescribe a round of antibiotics to see if some sinus congestion was hiding inside. During the round of antibiotics, the pressure did improve, but a small amount of pressure was still occurring. A sinus CT scan was ordered, and it came back all clear. The ENT recommended a neurologist as the next step.

However, I decided first to hit pause and see my primary care doctor because primary care can evaluate conditions and have insight into the best investigations or specialists based on symptoms. I was still wondering if something in my spine could be causing this face pressure since sitting seemed to trigger it. I did not know whether a neurologist would evaluate the spine or tell me I needed to see an orthopedic doctor.

I had wondered, even before this, if primary care would be the best for pursuing face pressure. But since I had already started talking with my physical medicine doctor about it and seeing him at regular intervals for spasticity, I felt I should stick with him in pursuing the face pressure. I had already discussed the subject quite a bit more with him than with primary care. I also feared that talking with two doctors about the same thing was dishonest because it was like setting one doctor up against another. Fast forward to when my need became greater than my fear, so I scheduled an appointment with my primary care doctor.

Back to the Pelvis Issue

Back when my physical medicine doctor ordered physical therapy for my pelvis, I did the familiar self-pep-talk of "I'm really going to do this and put all my effort into it." After the visits ended and I had gathered all the exercises, I set out with determination. I came upon the familiar, but forgotten, obstacle of the exercises increasing the spasticity in my body. This hurdle had been forgotten because when I had encountered it in the past, I had given up in defeat. I created a self-fulfilling prophecy that I couldn't get the help I needed because my disability was too complicated. This fulfilled prophecy was coupled with feelings of guilt and shame for giving up.

I had forgotten about the familiar obstacle of heightened spasticity because, in the past, I had retreated into the protection of my eating disorder. The eating disorder buried my guilt and shame and attempted to soothe my feelings of failure. We have all heard that we should keep going no matter what. I had never defined at what limit I should stop or pause to evaluate the situation. I had never set a boundary or taken the time to realize there is a healthy boundary. Thereby, I kept the door open for shame to come in. I also had not realized a person could seek another physical therapist, other therapy options, or find peace inside.

As the spasticity increased from these therapy exercises, my left hip felt even more unstable, and the twisting-pulling feeling increased, but I had no pain. Given my past history of hip dislocation, I became concerned about whether my hip could dislocate again. I wanted an x-ray. Imaging is what I had been wanting all along to evaluate the things going on in my body. I had even wanted an MRI of my right knee when I was concerned about it, but I never asked directly or brought it up in discussion because I assumed doctors automatically pursued investigations when needed and knew the best approaches to take.

I also assumed they knew every current orthopedic pathology in my body simply by observing my movements or reading my medical history. As a child, I went to doctors in Chicago, a top-rated location for orthopedic care and traumatic brain injuries. My parents voiced my problems to the doctors. I do not recall the words spoken in those conversations. There in my childhood, I developed the assumption that all doctors discern orthopedic problems just by seeing the patient move. When I was a child receiving orthopedic care, I trusted that all choices made about a patient's care were always the best.

As I grew older, I began to understand that doctors do not always make optimal choices. As a result, I developed a degree of mistrust in doctors for my future care, while I continued to hope to trust their care. I got stuck in a mixture of hope, trust, doubt, grief, fear, and despair. I left all of those thoughts and feelings inside, and I did not know I was stuck in them.

Due to a previous conversation with my physical medicine doctor about another malady with my right leg, in which he stated imaging was only needed when pain was present, I had resigned myself to the approach of no imaging with no pain, even though I did not agree with it. Now, with my concern about my hip, I began researching on the internet to build my case and state my argument as to why I needed an x-ray. I came across information that identified my gait pattern as the Trendelenberg gait. I continued researching and found an article that stated several conditions can cause that gait pattern, so the best approach is to perform an x-ray to identify the precise pathology. I was grateful and relieved to find the specific information I needed, which backed up my request for an x-ray.

I sat down to write a letter to my physical medicine doctor and send it through my patient portal. I stated my history of a dislocated hip and the surgery at seven years old that allowed the hip to go back into place. I included the link to the article and stated that the article recommends an x-ray to determine the pathology. I let him know

I would be seeing my primary care doctor later that week, and if he had the opportunity, he could coordinate with her to order the x-ray. Only later did I realize he might not see the letter before my primary care appointment. Nor had I told him the reason for my visit to my primary care; I was seeing her because of the pressure in my face.

That night, I had another school dream in which I was trying to find my classes. However, this dream was different. I finally went to the office to get a copy of my class schedule, even though only two weeks were left in the school year.

I woke up quite amazed by that dream. I knew it meant something good because in my dream, I went to the office and got a copy of my class schedule. After I had sent the letter to my physical medicine doctor the night before, I felt satisfied, confident, and relieved that I had truly expressed what had been in my heart all along: the truth of what I was experiencing in my body and how I felt it important to investigate its pathology in light of my medical history so I could have clear facts to help me weigh my decisions going forward.

When I saw my primary care doctor that week, I told her I had sent a letter to my physical medicine doctor regarding my concerns with my hip and leg, and I asked if she had heard from him. She had not. In light of the increased pulling sensation at the hip, she agreed an x-ray would be important, especially because of my pelvis's medical history. She was going to send a note to the physical medicine doctor.

Within a few days, I heard back from my physical medicine doctor, who ordered the requested x-ray of the pelvis. That x-ray showed I had a shallow acetabulum, or a shallow hip socket, which leads the femur ball to sit in the socket less securely than it would if it were fully formed.

The radiologist recommended further x-rays to evaluate the findings. Those x-rays were completed, and the report included a center angle measurement determining if hip dysplasia was present. The report stated my center angle is twenty-five degrees, which is at the very top or beginning of the pre-dysplasia range; the higher the number, the better. My physical medicine doctor explained that the shallowness was likely developmental because my bones were still growing at the time of the accident. Because of my disability, I engaged in fewer weight-bearing activities in childhood than usual. Weight-bearing activities help the hip socket develop.

I was still concerned about whether the hip was in any danger of dislocating, so my physical medicine doctor supplied a referral to an orthopedic surgeon. Upon examination of my hip, the orthopedic doctor believed the joint was secure and not in danger of dislocation. I felt relieved that the hip was secure and could continue shaping my life without fearing dislocation.

At the same time the hip evaluation was happening, my primary care doctor had also ordered a cervical spine MRI to evaluate the face pressure. She said problems in the cervical spine can cause pressure sensations in the face and numbness in the hands, like I was experiencing. The MRI showed no pinched nerves but mild bulging at C4-C5 and C6-C7 and arthritis in several vertebrae. My doctor said the pressure in my face and numbness in my hands were due to the arthritis irritating the cranial nerves leading to my face and hands. I was grateful to finally have an explanation. The information gave me reassurance that when I experience pressure in my face, it is not life-threatening. Rather, those nerves are solely sensation nerves causing the facial sensations.

I have found that exercises for the shoulders and neck keep the pressure away. If I experience pressure, I need to do more of those exercises or adjust my seated posture. I feel empowered in a new way by exercises and have gained a new appreciation for those exercises. Physical therapy exercises for me always had the purpose of improving movement, balance, and mobility instead of treating pain because I had no pain. The exercises either produced little to no gains or aggravated the spastic muscles. My result was frustration and an unfriendly relationship with physical therapy exercises. However, experiencing pain relief with my neck and hands has given me a new appreciation for therapy exercises and their benefits even beyond pain relief.

The Eyes of the Beholder

All of these breakthroughs were taking place in November/December 2021. That same December, I went to my optometrist for my annual eye checkup. Historically, I have had dry eye syndrome since the age of thirty, which was treated with prescription eye drops, artificial tears, and attempts with punctual plugs that fell out. Early on, an ophthalmologist informed me dry eye syndrome can produce corneal scarring that can be addressed if it occurs. Over the years, my vision started getting worse and blotchy due to the scarring, leading to frustration and anxiety because it was affecting my balance, and the vision battle was reducing the power and energy I possessed to address the mobility challenge.

I began to have difficulty obtaining an accurate eyeglass prescription. I set out on a quest to find an eye doctor who could help me. Around 2012, an occupational therapist suggested I try an optometrist in Fort Wayne who was good with complex vision problems. I went to the doctor in Fort Wayne and obtained a successful eyeglass prescription. She also told me she estimated I'd be eligible for a corneal transplant in five years.

I returned to her the following year and experienced the same problem I had experienced in the past with an eyeglass prescription that did not work for me. I decided Fort Wayne was too far to travel back and forth to if I needed reexaminations for prescription adjustments, so I sought a practice closer to home.

I chose a doctor and received an accurate prescription that worked for me the first year. In the second year, the prescription did not work. I decided to go to her predecessor to seek out available interventions. I asked him what I could do about my vision. He said my right eye was 20/80 and my left eye was 20/30; together, they were 20/35. He told me I should be thankful I could see that well because he had patients with vision worse than mine. His remedy was to continue using eye drops.

I retreated in my quest for help, feeling I was being too forward and perhaps impatient in seeking intervention. So, I settled in with another optometrist, thinking the medical field consensus was that I was just supposed to endure. I resigned myself to believing the doctor would send me to a specialist when it was the right time. I stopped going back to the eye doctor for prescription adjustments when my eyes could not adapt to new prescriptions because making repeated attempts became too tiring and disappointing.

In October 2020, I consulted with a neuro-optometrist to explore the option of vision therapy for nystagmus, a condition where the eyes involuntarily move in irregular patterns. I hoped that addressing nystagmus would help me endure my vision. The situation turned out to be challenging due to my own anxiety during that point in my life. The doctor and I set out first to get an eyeglass prescription because I had resigned myself, at that point, to wearing over-the-counter readers. He gave me a prescription that caused immediate headaches and dizziness when I put them on. His office recommended giving my eyes two weeks to adjust to the glasses, but the side effects were too intense to try. My anxiety with vision and mobility was so high at that point that I could not make myself return to his office. Plus, the structure of the practitioner's entrance created complications for getting my walker through, and the obstacle seemed like a mountain at that time.

Since I could not make myself go back there, I decided to see my regular optometrist for an eyeglass prescription and enquire about the possibility of referring me to a specialist who could address my scarring condition. I saw her in December 2020. She said she usually sends patients to Indianapolis (three hours away) for corneal conditions. She could refer me, but she did not think my vision was bad enough yet that they would do anything. I decided if they weren't going to do anything, I would wait since there was no point in taking the time and effort to make the trip.

A year later, in December 2021, which was soon after the final dream, I returned to my optometrist for my annual exam. She said the scarring was covering my field of vision, and she could no longer get a prescription reading. It was time to refer me to a specialist. She shared that Indianapolis is where she usually sends patients, but there was also a doctor at Great Lakes Eye Care with an office in Mishawaka, Indiana (about thirty minutes away). I chose the closer option.

Great Lakes Eye Care called me the next day, and in under a week, I saw their corneal specialist. What ensued in 2022 was four trips to the surgery center in St. Joseph, Michigan, and a number of in-office, follow-up visits. The surgery center visits included corneal scrapings on both eyes, as well as punctal cauteries on both upper tear ducts.

The result was delightfully clear vision and significant improvement of dry eye syndrome.

I like to believe God summons the powers of his universe to work on our behalf. After I started speaking up about my needs and my thoughts about my hip to the physical medicine doctor, God confirmed I was on a right path through completing the eighteen-month recurring dream in which I finally went to the school office and got a copy of my class schedule. At the same time I spoke up about my hip, I spoke up about my facial discomfort and hand numbness. The primary care doctor stepped in and helped me with that, in addition to her support with the pelvis.

The cervical arthritis diagnosis from the MRI also finally gave me the evidence I needed to get a bone density scan approved by my insurance. The bone density scan confirmed osteopenia. The osteopenia diagnosis arms me and my doctors with the knowledge needed to tend to the condition. Perhaps my speaking up in 2020 to enquire about a specialist for my eyes was good practice for the breakthrough events to come in 2021 when my voice became untethered.

Interestingly, I joined a book coaching program in November 2022. My final visit with the corneal specialist was December 9 of that year. My tenure with the eye specialist and surgeries brought physical, mental, and spiritual healing. The books in my dreams are still an intriguing piece that spark curiosity as to whether they pointed to writing a book. At any rate, life is a beautiful tapestry that weaves together its known and unknown mysteries.

I have been fascinated and awed by dreams since I was twenty-one. The Bible was the foundation that inspired my interest. It contains several accounts of dreams and their interpretations. I've always loved the story in Daniel 10, where Daniel fasted and prayed, and God sent his angel to war in the heavens to break through and deliver the answer to Daniel. I believe God does that for each of us when we ask and keep asking, seek and keep seeking, knock and keep knocking. When we keep believing, we keep seeking, we keep learning, we keep growing, and we keep standing firm. We remain flexible and curious in awe and wonder. We can become focused on expecting a little answer, but our Creator has the power to answer in ways that are much bigger than we ever thought or imagined.

I never imagined a year and a half of fascinating dreams culminating in a message that has led to breakthroughs in the care of my physical body, the health of my mind, and the growth of my spirit. It was a message given to me about the power of my voice. The power of speaking up and giving voice to the thoughts and needs inside of us. The power of speaking up and sharing the dreams, goals, and aspirations within you. The power of speaking up and giving voice to the knowledge and inspirations that light fires within your soul. This power is the power of your untethered voice.

One last thing—in the final dream when I went to the office to get a copy of my class schedule, I've pondered what it meant by *there were still two weeks left in the school year*. I just realized it was a message saying that *it is never too late*. I leave you with that encouragement—*It is never too late.*

Discussion

1. If you explore the interpretation of dreams, share why you do it, or how it fulfills or excites you. If you would rather not explore dream interpretation, share any of your thoughts, or even fears, about interpreting dreams.

_____

_____

_____

_____

2. If you have felt like people do not understand you or understand your concerns, what additional thoughts or details can you share with them to express your view more clearly?

_____

_____

_____

_____

3. Is there any situation or goal that makes you feel, "It's too late," or "I'm too old"? What would happen if you realized it is not too late and you are not too old?

_____

_____

_____

_____

Poem

Your Untethered Voice

Your Untethered Voice
It came from within,
A healing of
Your soul.

Your Untethered Voice,
Written by choice
So the world
Might know.

The untethered voices
Have peered into their mortality
Unto a clear view
Of their reality.

They have touched and beheld
Their fragile humanity.
They have seen their sacred essence.
They've found the power of gravity,

The grounding that keeps
Them centered.
They take charge
Of what does enter.

They seek to speak clearly
To be understood,
To express thoughts thoroughly,
To accomplish the good.

To heal
To break barriers
To seal
To build up.

They've discovered the joy
Of their passions
And give permission
To be fulfilled.

May the sun rise upon you
From morning unto night,
In daylight and in darkness
May you always have sight.

Chapter 7
Exploring the Truths
of Disability's Challenges

D ISABILITY COMES IN MANY FORMS, such as physical disabilities, learning disabilities, and mental disabilities. Each one brings their challenges. In this chapter, I speak of some of the challenges I've faced as well as some of the challenges I know others have encountered.

Growing up, I cringed to hear my voice on a tape recorder. It was quiet, raspy, and slow. I simply avoided listening to it. I also avoided viewing myself walking. I looked away when passing by mirrors. I glanced to the side when approaching the glass doors of stores, ignoring my reflection. I felt subtly justified in rejecting my appearance. I thought it was okay, and I was sure I was not the only one who rejected their appearance. Like the other things I buried, I buried my self-rejection. I reasoned, "If I bury it, I can ignore it." I thought life could continue just fine with all of the visible treasures, and we could ignore the buried hardships and secrets.

But life does not work that way. We cannot be whole when parts of us are buried. A more profound truth is that when we bury hard things, we also bury treasures. It is impossible to justify our rejection of our own selves. We are the ones who suffer. In turn, the world suffers. We must access the compassion within ourselves to begin loving the parts of our bodies and souls we reject. When we place a hand of compassion on those parts, we begin to see acceptance blossom. As acceptance continues to bloom, love pours out upon those parts, and we become whole.

Ataxia/Balance

My brain injury left me with ataxia, a disruption of balance and coordination. I learned to walk independently without the aid of a cane or walker, but the challenge to avoid falls was always present. Keeping my balance required concentration. Sometimes, at gatherings, I desired to mingle and be more social, but I felt more secure staying in one place or keeping ambulation minimal. As a result, I sometimes chastised myself for not making the effort to go to another room to join in with a group of people and for being lazy or rude. I never looked deeper to discover my apprehension to move was my subconscious mind saying, "I don't feel safe walking."

Instead of recognizing and admitting I did not feel safe, I sometimes encouraged myself to be brave. "You can do it," I told myself before I walked across the room, or I would strategize the best path to get where I wanted to go. When striving to gain independent mobility, we must look closely at our level of feeling safe. A person without ataxia may have no problem feeling secure if their legs are strong enough to walk. But the balance problems of ataxia present an extra layer of difficulty. I'd had a balance challenge since I was five years old, and I did not know it was not ordinary. I did not recognize I was dizzy. When I started seeking help in my early forties for my declining balance, I had heard dizziness described as room-spinning. I answered no when asked if I was dizzy because the room did not spin. At about age forty-nine or fifty, a doctor asked me, "Is it like rocking on a boat?" My answer was, "Yes!" It was a relief to have the right words to describe it finally.

I encourage providers to ask questions to help patients describe their problems. Sometimes, we do not know how to articulate what we are experiencing. If a patient has had a disability since childhood, some challenges may get labeled in their mind as normal because years ago, when they were a child, their child mind labeled things as normal that were not. Therefore, they may not know their challenge is a verifiable problem, or they may not know how to express it.

To those with a disability, stay in tune with the messages your mind and subconscious mind send you. Whether you have ataxia or not, if you are walking independently but don't feel safe, evaluate what steps you could take to feel safer. Are you dizzy? Either room-spinning dizzy or boat-rocking dizzy? Would physical therapy to make your legs stronger be the answer? Would a cane or a walker help? If you need assistance evaluating your thoughts and needs, talk with a medical provider to aid your analysis. It is essential to feel safe rather than leave the problem unaddressed and possibly put your subconscious mind into fight-or-flight mode without knowing it.

Walking independently is highly valued and widely promoted. Walking is one of the best avenues of exercise and activity to give the body the movement it needs to be healthy. In addition to physical benefits, a healthy body that can move well contributes to mental health, both physiologically with endorphins and psychologically with the joys of moving, going, accomplishing, doing, and doing with ease. If you cannot walk, any safe movements and exercises are valuable because they provide physiological and psychological benefits.

Until eleventh grade, I fell quite a bit at school, on average about twice a week. When I fell, the load of books I was carrying would often go sprawling across the floor. Almost always, someone nearby would help me up and help pick up my books. I would proceed on my way, processing embarrassment, sadness, and disappointment, but mostly stuffing those emotions down.

One day, however, when I fell and someone helped me up, I felt the power of compassion in a way I had not allowed myself to feel before. At that moment, I knew exactly what the Bible was talking about metaphorically when it spoke of pouring in the oil and the wine.

"But a certain Samaritan, as he journeyed, came where he was: and when he saw him, he had compassion on him, and went to him, and bound up his wounds, pouring in oil and wine, and set him on his own beast, and brought him to an inn, and took care of him."

— Luke 10:33-34 KJV

At that instant, I felt the healing power of compassion pour into my soul like the oil and the wine. I've carried that powerful lesson with me ever since: the lesson that our acts of compassion can be the healing oil someone needs.

My balance improved by eleventh grade, so I did not fall as often. I believe a regimen of riding an exercise bike contributed to that decrease. Exercise does indeed help with balance. People I've been acquainted with in social media groups have also stated that they have experienced balance improvements with exercise.

Exercise can help balance problems, but it is not the cure-all for them. Therefore, we want to be careful about believing we can cure and heal every balance challenge if we just work hard enough. I point this out because I've ex-perienced self-judgment with my own past rigidity mind-set; it caused me to berate myself for not doing enough and getting confused about what would help my body. Exercise will help different people to different degrees, and the degree may increase or decrease at different times in life because the body and balance are so complex.

Brain injuries and disabilities are complex in their pat-terns of signal interruption, so much so that we have to give ourselves grace. We can experiment, test methods and therapies, and do the work. Still, we also need to allow space for grace to acknowledge and accept the things we cannot change, whether the things are things our bodies are not capable of achieving or whether those things are possibilities that will take so much time and vitality to test that the efforts will derail us from the innate strengths that will fulfill us and become gifts to the world. The truths of our abilities and passions will set us free to live fulfilling lives.

Disability requires an extra layer of self-knowledge and self-compassion to find our self-acceptance and ful-fillment. This layer has been renewed and clarified for me through healing. The extra layer becomes a strength that will get tested and flexed for the rest of our lives. The more we know ourselves, the more precisely we know our yes-es, nos, and maybes. We can more quickly discern that yes, I can do that, or no, I can't do that. The can'ts become cans because we either find a way to do it or harness the power to redirect our energy and focus on attainable possibilities.

Mobility Aids

As we age, whether physically disabled or not, many of us will face the realities of mobility aids, whether for ourselves or loved ones. We will begin to notice the struc-tural barriers in our homes and society as we use these aids. For example, when we use a cane for mobility, we see minimal barriers, depending on our level of need. We can maneuver in places reasonably well with a cane. If we use a walker, we begin to see more barriers. A walker takes up more space in a room and when going through doorways. It is also more difficult to transport when going out. Whether the user can transport the walker themselves depends on their strength and balance level to get the walker in and out of the vehicle. A ramp for entering and exiting the house may still be optional when using a walker depending on factors such as the number of stair steps, if a person can maneuver stairsteps, or if someone else will be helping the individual lift their walker in and out of the house.

When considering a wheelchair, we may have to make some changes in the home, such as rearranging furniture and building access ramps. Traveling to places will require someone to help get the wheelchair in and out of the vehicle or an automobile equipped with a wheelchair ramp or lift. In addition to structural and handling concerns, a wheelchair lift or a wheelchair van adds a heavy cost burden upon a disabled person or their caregivers. Lifts are sometimes the preferred option because they are less expensive, ranging from $1,000-$15,000. Currently, modifications to a van for a wheelchair with a ramp can range from $10,000-$30,000. This modification cost is on top of the vehicle price.

The equipping price varies widely based on the devices needed for each case. Automobile lenders often will not finance the cost of the equipment, so people with disabilities are left to find their own means of covering the price or to check with their health insurance. Health insurance plans may cover the cost of vehicle modifications, an option worth considering. Government-funded traditional Medicare does not cover modifications, but some Medicare

Advantage Plans may. Specific Medicaid programs may also cover adaptive customizations. Grants or non-profit organizations in your state may also assist with the costs. If people cannot find financial assistance or obtain cash through savings or earnings, they are left to utilize home equity loans, credit cards, crowdfunding, or other fundraisers. Any out-of-pocket costs paid for modifications are tax deductible.

People who cannot afford a wheelchair van or lift must find family, friends, hired help, or some kind of public or private paid accessible transportation. The total price of the fee-for-service transit can be expensive, with charges accumulating per mile round trip. To help with this expense, Medicaid has a transportation benefit that provides coverage for individuals to and from medical appointments. Not every Medicaid recipient knows about this benefit. Medicare is starting to step up to the challenge of meeting this need through some of its Medicare Advantage Plans. If a person is interested in that option, they can examine the different plans to see which ones offer the benefit. In addition, your local Council on Aging may provide reduced-cost transportation for those who meet income qualifications.

Nystagmus

Nystagmus is a condition where the eyes move rapidly and uncontrollably in horizontal, vertical, or circular patterns. It can produce dizziness, blurred or double vision, and tilted head positioning. Tilted head positioning can occur when the brain is trying to compensate for the eye movements. Tilting slows the movements. Prisms can be added to eyeglass prescriptions to improve visual acuity and eliminate head tilt.

Nystagmus sometimes results from traumatic brain injuries. It did in my case. I did not realize I had nystagmus or double vision until I was an adult. Just as the balance issue became normal to me, the double vision did as well. I did not realize I saw double, and doctors never brought it up. Looking back, I recognize I was tested for it during my eye exams, but it was never named. My double is not two whole objects side by side or one above the other; rather, it is an overlapping with the top one slightly above and diagonally to the left.

The prism prescription I have has not completely eliminated my double vision. My new optometrist recently explained I have binocular suppression. Binocular suppression is the brain's subconscious suppression of parts of vision from one eye to try to eliminate the discomfort of seeing double. He explained the suppression makes getting an accurate prism reading difficult. I'm continually amazed by new revelations about aspects of my condition that have been present for years. This explained to me why, over the years, when I went to the eye doctor and participated in the test of reporting at what point two objects lined up side-by-side on the screen, I would see two objects, but lose sight of two and only see one before they reached alignment. I believe the suppression also causes difficulty for me during refractive eye exams because I often have to ask the doctor to repeat the lenses because I cannot detect the difference. These tests would make me nervous when I went to eye doctor appointments and apologetic for asking them to repeat the lenses or alignment test. Knowing years earlier about binocular suppression in my visual experience would have eliminated the emotional distress of feeling like I had failed or was deficient. It is pretty amazing to learn they possibly knew all along what was going on. It also indicates that I can benefit from asking more questions about my concerns and even speaking up about emotional discomfort.

Single-Handed

From the time of the accident at five years old, I had to learn how to accomplish tasks with mostly my right hand. My left hand has about 10-20 percent function. To use my left hand to hold objects, I have to place those objects in that hand with my right hand. I can sometimes grasp stationary objects, such as the handle on specific mixing bowls, pitchers, or lever doorknobs, but I have to take extra time to do it.

I've adapted several tasks in order to accomplish them. Buttoning with one hand is so automatic now that I rarely think about it. I learned that skill in occupational therapy when I was five. Buttoning my right sleeve on a long-sleeved shirt is an undertaking I cannot accomplish in the typical way. To wear the shirt, I either button the right sleeve before I put it on and then squeeze my right hand through, or I use a buttoning aid that has a hook. In recent years, I simply seldom wear long-sleeved shirts with sleeves that button. Zipping a coat is a task I accomplish with both hands. However, I have to place the left end of the zipper into my left hand and then do all the rest of the work with my right hand. It takes time.

Embarrassment

People with disabilities may face embarrassment about their challenges. I can share insights on the extra mental hurdles a disabled person might have to process as someone watches them adaptively accomplish tasks. The differently-abled may be processing embarrassment about doing the procedure differently or taking longer than usual. We may even be sad or concerned about holding you or others up while you wait on us. Or we may have already processed our embarrassment and sadness and are simply truly grateful you are exercising the patience to wait on us. We feel your love and acceptance.

Sometimes, we may or may not prefer help. Preference for no assistance may result from confidence that we can do the task ourselves. If we reject offers of assistance because of grief or embarrassment, we can look deeper to find why. We can discern our deeper need, heal the why, and then step into the place of love in our hearts to be able to love ourselves and others and receive offers of help with gratitude when we need it.

The more things we can do ourselves and the more precisely we can find the balance between aid and independence, the more we can thrive and continue maintaining that independence. Less activity can certainly lead to less ability to remain physically strong and flexible, but when those reduced-activity challenges arise, we do not have to face them alone or in fear.

Sometimes, the load does get heavy, and extra support can renew our strength. We can accept help in love or gratefully say, "No, thank you." And if that zipper is not cooperating and you feel frustrated, have compassion for yourself and ask for assistance.

Finding Assistance

Disability can be acquired in various ways, whether permanent or temporary, whether born with it or acquired through accident or disease, whether incurred while recovering from surgery or injury, or experienced through aging decline. If faced with a disability and we encounter things we cannot do, it is important to get help. We may need a broad range of assistance, including housekeeping, transportation, personal care, and mental health support.

Supporting mental and emotional health is a crucial component when someone is facing challenges. This support allows a person to stay stronger both physically and mentally. Housekeeping, transportation, and personal care are needs that definitely support mental health. It is important to reach out for assistance if you are struggling to take care of yourself, your house, or your transportation needs.

Procuring assistance is one of the extra challenges of disability. Efforts to find available transportation and arrange all of the details can be stressful. The same goes for housekeeping or any other assistance. We hear stories of people getting help through home care agencies, but not receiving care because the agency was short-staffed. We can also sometimes experience interruptions in care from privately hired help. A good idea is to have more than one person you can call on for a backup plan in case of unexpected absence of the usual caregiver. The most important key is for us to love ourselves enough to pursue getting the help we need. If the task of contacting yet another person or searching for yet another solution seems too hard, it can help to pause, take a deep breath, and remind yourself you are doing this because you love yourself and help is what you need.

Too Much Help

The question of when to get and not to get help can be confusing if we have doubts whether we need it. The more we can do for ourselves, the more we nurture and maintain our physical, mental, and emotional health. At the same time, accepting help from others can foster our good health and be a gift to ourselves and others. When choosing, we should look at what is best. Therefore, we consider whether this help will benefit or hinder us. We are the ones who can best define yes or no and allow the flexibility to continue to determine what does and does not work in the future. We must define our path from a place of self-love, self-acceptance, and trust. Those who fear focusing on oneself and that receiving from others leads to selfishness are examining the thought through a place of confused logic. We may also be obsessed with the concept that giving is better than receiving. We, thereby, remove ourselves from receiving love and the wisdom to balance our needs within our circumstances. To overcome that fear of receiving and acknowledging our needs, we must move past logic and reach into our spirit, the place of truth. Spirit is where we will find love, acceptance, and trust.

Benefits of Support Groups

In my mid-forties, I discovered Facebook was rife with support groups. A person can find a support group there for just about anything. I joined a couple of support groups for cerebral palsy, a support group for traumatic brain injuries, and even a support group for strokes since a stroke causes injury to the brain. I began to realize the power of support groups and the power of connections with people experiencing similar things. There is an understanding, a feeling of being seen and heard, a feeling that someone gets exactly what I mean because they have experienced the same thing. You learn from others and others learn from you; you discover different approaches or views you never thought of before; you learn of new technologies and tools, and you gain some of the support you need to navigate this area of your life.

I discovered that many people with cerebral palsy experience an earlier onset of mobility decline than non-disabled people. The early decline is common. On average, it begins around age forty, but for some sooner, some later. A general fear surrounds the decline—fear of what life will be like in the future with decreased mobility, and a quest to find the tools and methods to prevent this decline. It's the same quest the non-disabled face in later years.

Since I joined the online cerebral palsy support groups, I've witnessed many discussions about mobility decline. The comments of people who have said they made the choice to use a wheelchair because it allowed them to better accomplish the things important to them really stuck out to me. I realized my mind was trying to process that very thing. The younger they were when they made the decision to use a wheelchair, the more they stuck out to me. At first, I stood back at a distance, wondering how they did that. Is it possible? Is it right? As I came closer, I began to admire them for having the ability to know themselves and the confidence to make the decision that gave them the power to pursue their goals and dreams.

The optional choice of using a wheelchair is purely an individual thing. It is based on your body's abilities, your ability to decide how much therapy, work, or activity you can put into maintaining mobility, your amount of pain if any pain is present, and at what point you say "enough." It is also influenced by your goals and dreams. If you want to keep walking and you feel that walking serves you best because it feels good to be able to freely open the door, step outside, open the car door, get right in, and go, then that is terrific. However, if you feel a wheelchair allows you to more freely get out the door, get into your vehicle, and go places, that is incredible, too. If you feel a wheelchair would allow you to get around your house better, take care of housework more efficiently, have more energy to do exercises, or take care of yourself, that is important. The feeling of freedom, independence, and the capacity to get around is what we are aiming for.

If you struggle in making your decision, remember, wheelchair use does not have to be full-time. You can opt to use it part-time. It all depends on your needs and desires. As with a cane and a walker, when I contemplated using a wheelchair, my first inclination was, "Oh no, using that means I'm quickly declining or going downhill." Then I realized, "No, wait a minute; many people use canes, walkers, or wheelchairs for years, even lifelong. And they are out there happily living life. So, why should I think it's the end of all things good and that it means I and life decline? It doesn't!" We need to have these conversations with ourselves and remove the fear of decreased mobility because life does not end simply because of mobility decline.

Mental Health

After studying OCD, perfectionism, and eating disorders, I realized how disability played a role in the mix for me as well. I recognize that disability or chronic illness of any sort—diabetes, cancer, heart disease, etc.—presents extra challenges to mental health. Society would benefit if we, parents, educators, medical professionals, employers, and even politicians took note of this situation and participated in avenues of awareness, compassion, and aid. We can all be our own best keepers and advocates when in a healthy mental and emotional state. In that state, we have the power to raise our own voices and seek help. But if we bury or miss our own needs, are unaware of our needs' importance, or are hindered by mental, emotional, or physical unwellness, then the need is critical for the compassionate discernment of others to step in and help. If others don't know how to recognize these needs, they aren't aware of the lifelines their intervention can bring. Many organizations hold awareness campaigns you can get involved in to help spread the word about areas you are interested in. The National Eating Disorders Association (NEDA) for eating disorders, and BeThe1To for suicide prevention are just a couple of examples. You can search the websites of causes you are interested in and look for tools and resources to find how you can help. Together, we can create awareness and inspire compassion to take action.

I've walked through a few periods of clinical depression as a result of not adequately addressing the challenges of disability and other needs. Unaddressed challenges and needs become overwhelming. I encourage anyone with a disability to stay connected to community and support. Connect with medical providers, social service providers, friends nearby, friends across the globe, groups through social media, or groups through other virtual meetings. We have so many resources available in this day and age. Utilize them and keep seeking when you have needs until you find the resources that help you meet them or heal the wounds of heartache. Every person can find their place of thriving and fulfillment and continue walking in that place. It's a place with self-love as its foundation. It's where we reach into our core to know ourselves truly. As our discoveries blossom inside amid honesty and truth, they produce joy and fulfillment that spills out into the world because we are engaging in the things that are good and fulfilling for us. That joy makes us want to love others as we love ourselves and inspire them to love themselves, too, so their joy and fulfillment can overflow.

Because I've gained my voice and have learned more about myself, I can now make more confident decisions and engage in dialogue with my providers about my needs, desires, and perceptions, and I can work with them to shape the path I want to take.

By exploring the fact that disability has challenges, discussing our mental window of tolerance, and being aware that we can experience both mental and physiological responses when we become overwhelmed, we can hopefully take steps to respond to ourselves with compassion when we face decisions about the best course of action to support our needs and goals.

In whatever area where we need to decide what serves us best—whether walking, using a wheelchair, making home renovations to accommodate a disability, or getting help for household or personal care—let's make our decisions with self-compassion. In turn, we can view others with compassion who are facing those decisions.

Discussion

1. Recall a time someone helped you and their care stood out like a healing balm or aid that touched your heart in an extra-special way.

_____

_____

_____

_____

2. Do you feel safe and stable while walking?

_____

_____

_____

_____

3. Have you evaluated your balance or discussed a balance evaluation with your doctor?

_____

_____

_____

_____

4. If you use mobility aids, have you addressed any structural barriers or challenges in your home that make using your device more difficult?

_____

_____

_____

_____

5. If someone in your home or extended family uses mobility aids, have you supported them in addressing structural barriers or challenges?

_____

_____

_____

_____

6. If you or someone in your household uses a walker or wheelchair, have you made space for transportation accommodations? If not, what is your first step in addressing the accommodation need?

_____

_____

_____

_____

7. What questions about your concerns have you not asked your providers that may be beneficial to ask?

_____

_____

_____

_____

8. List ways someone can support a person facing physical or mental challenges.

_____

_____

_____

_____

Poems

Living in the Overflow

Living in the overflow,
Creating a new song,
Touching the compassion,
No longer feeling wrong.

Accepting all that is
Born and birthed within.
Reaching to the core,
Uniting truth again.

Knowing now your yes and no.
Seeing your clear path.
Noting hardest mysteries
Were solved when you did ask.

Winding paths ahead,
Mountains yet to climb,
And they all are conquered
With unity and time.

Feasting in the overflow,
Joy and love divine,
With passion and with purpose.
Come now; it's our mealtime.

Move to Live

The bridled joy
The strings attached
The weighty moves
The hardened paths.

Reaching deep
Reaching far
Grabbing hold
Of who you are.

The desires reside
In your soul
To move, to create,
That's the goal.

Setting forth
The determined stride
The decision made
Not to hide.

The body moves.
The body works.
Life proceeds.
New moments birthed.

Step Into Your Shoes

Step into your shoes,
The shoes that say *you*.
The shoes that are true
And confidently on cue.

Step into your shoes,
The shoes that bear your name.
The shoes now in the game,
Dancing fully when it rains.

Step into your shoes,
The shoes that change the world.
Walking paths now unfurled,
Speaking truth-empowered words.

Chapter 8
Transforming Disability

A LL FORMS OF DISABILITY UNDOUBTEDLY come with disadvantages. I would be dishonest if I said balance struggles with falls, accomplishing tasks, and maneuvering in a wheelchair, or even walking with a walker carry no challenges. We can all imagine the ease of operating throughout each day with a body and mind fully functioning optimally, able to bend, lift, run, jump, type, speak, and process information with no hindrances.

I spent my life trying to be normal, sometimes feeling the awkwardness and embarrassment of a body that functioned differently in motion—motion with a limp, falls, and my walking path sometimes veering to the left. At school, church, or social gatherings when everyone was to take the hand of the person next to them, as someone grabbed my left hand, I would think, *I hope my hand does not tighten up so that they think I'm squeezing their hand.* That anxious thought would trigger my hand to tighten, and conscious efforts to loosen the hand only made it squeeze tighter. I would feel uncomfortable and embarrassed, wondering what the person thought. I did explain my predicament a few times, but that was rare. For the most part, I remained uncomfortable and embarrassed.

In my moments of embarrassment, I told myself, *Oh, that is silly to feel embarrassed.* I would try to brush it aside by burying it. *The Merriam-Webster Dictionary* defines embarrassment as "feeling a state of self-conscious confusion or distress." *Psychology Today* says embarrassment is a form of social feedback that triggers emotions of guilt, shame, awkwardness, self-consciousness, and vulnerability that make us want to avoid making the same mistake again. However, if a person's mistake is due to something they cannot change, such as a disability, the emotion can become grief and shame that they cannot change their body. Whether disabled or not, we all encounter embarrassment and can benefit by identifying strategies to process and handle our emotions.

As with any emotion, we can first realize that emotions are not permanent. An emotion only lasts for ninety seconds and then leaves our body. Our thoughts are what keep our emotions around longer. If we keep playing the story over in our heads, the emotion will stay as long as we continue ruminating about it. With this in mind, we can choose to let the emotion pass through and let the thoughts subside, too. We can also use a few other strategies to cope with our embarrassment.

Strategies for Coping with Embarrassment

- **Create a Helpful Statement:** If embarrassment overwhelms you, one strategy is to create a helpful statement of positive reinforcement, such as, "You've got this!"
- **Take a Few Deep Breaths:** Another approach is to take a few deep breaths to calm your body and bring you back into your center.
- **Speak to Yourself as If Speaking to a Friend:** A third good strategy is to speak to yourself with words of comfort and encouragement the same

way you'd talk to a friend who had just gotten embarrassed.

- **Journal About Your Feelings:** A fourth strategy is journaling about your feelings. Journaling is a great way to get feelings down on paper and then read them back to yourself to identify ways to speak kindness to yourself.

If you are struggling to cope with your feelings of embarrassment on your own, do not hesitate to reach out to a friend. We have all felt embarrassed, so your friend will understand your feelings. You are not alone.

I don't get embarrassed as much as I used to. I think time, experience, wisdom, and healing self-worth reduce our number of encounters with embarrassment. When we are more confident that we are who we are, we can celebrate ourselves, celebrate others, and help them celebrate who they are. I've learned to recognize embarrassment. When I encounter it now, I use it as a tool to look deeper to help me polish self-acceptance.

Disability transforms into a strength in the midst of self-compassion and self-awareness. We can replace and heal the negative thoughts and inner wounds when we become aware of them. The process of awareness, exchange, and healing takes time. That is why we move into our land through a journey, with each of us creating our own journey. The unhealthy thoughts and emotions of non-disabled individuals, whatever they may be, can also be transformed.

We transform ourselves and one another by ending comparison and accepting who we are and all of the treasures we hold inside. We strengthen ourselves and others by living in and sharing our treasures. By building our foundations with these treasures and gemstones, we may soon find ourselves fashioning and walking upon inner streets of gold because our land is rich and nourished. After paving our own streets inside with gold, we also begin to pave the streets around us, and we each begin to enrich the world one person at a time. I can testify that I have been transformed many times by the inner riches of others.

Society Benefits

Disabilities can cultivate unique perspectives and strengths in individuals with these challenges. Disabled people may possess enhanced problem-solving skills due to finding innovative ways of accomplishing goals and daily tasks in a world not always designed with their needs in mind. In the workplace and society, they can offer a deep understanding of accessibility issues. People with disabilities may also possess resilience, adaptability, and determination.

For example, consider what happens physiologically when a person becomes blind or visually impaired. Their brain reorganizes information and recruits other parts of the brain to create enhanced tactile perception, sound localization, and route learning. If the electricity went out in the middle of the night, the visually impaired person could get to another room better than their sighted family members because of enhanced route learning. This particular circuitry in the brain can also increase memory skills.

A study published in the *Journal of Psychological Science* shows people with autism spectrum disorder have superior visual-spatial skills and attention to detail. People with autism also possess honesty and integrity. They often perceive and interpret the world in unique ways that lend freshness, creativity, and new ideas. They also tend to be strong in logical thinking and problem-solving. In autism and all disabilities, we identify and celebrate the strengths of the person and give support to the individual's unique challenges.

Understanding Aging Challenges and Inclusion

When I was in my teens or twenties, I used to think it odd that references lumped together aging and disability. By my thirties, I realized the wisdom of categorizing them together because the aging and disabled face some of the same challenges. The lifelong or younger onset disabled may offer a unique empathy and understanding to the aging. When it becomes difficult for the aging to get up stairs, we've been there; when you need a shower chair to bathe safely, we've been there; when you need to start using a cane, walker, or wheelchair, we've been there, and we've experienced the fears and created the mind shifts needed to make those adjustments. We understand. And we can also offer the wisdom that life doesn't end there. It is possible to adjust to those new things and continue leading happy lives.

Aging is a global human truth. It is a reality we all face if we live long enough to achieve it. Those with disabilities can tell you about the structural features in the home and community that are valuable to mobility challenges. We can relate to the aging with empathy when they begin to experience some of aging's difficulties.

When I lived in an apartment in my early thirties, the landlord installed grab bars in the bathtub at my request. They were not yet a necessity that determined whether or not I could get into the bathtub, but I found using them provided extra peace of mind and assurance of safety. Later, when considering building a house, my aunt recommended building an accessible home. I saw the wisdom in her recommendation, but I was reluctant to view myself as one at the point of needing accessibility features, and I feared that making my home accessible before required would permit me to allow myself to decline. I was thirty-six at the time, viewing the possibility of accessibility needs being off in the future with a we'll-address-it-when-we-get-there approach.

During the construction of our house, we made some changes to our floor plan that saved our builder money. Our builder proposed using what we saved by those changes to make the primary bedroom and bath doorways the thirty-six-inch accessible standard. Even barring accessibility needs, we realized these wider doorways had the practical application of added ease for moving furniture in and out of rooms.

A couple of years after we moved into our new house, I had grab bars installed in the shower. Soon, I thought of other places in the house where a grab bar could benefit my needs because I discovered they were useful not only in the bathroom but in other areas. We have placed grab bars beside our exit doors, and I use them to steady myself as I step in and out. We have also put them outside the bathrooms and other doorways for my use, which also has proved helpful for getting up from the floor after I've gotten down to clean or sort something. Grab bars come in several colors, shapes, and styles, so I purchased ones that match our décor, and now we have grab bars throughout our house. The method I used to choose where to place grab bars was simply to sense where I felt extra steadying would benefit.

Some years ago, I started hearing the term *aging in place* regarding home features. Contrary to my earlier fears, I've discovered that accessibility features do not attract physical decline. Instead, they enhance life with their benefits. People often install accessibility features at the last minute in times of dire need. If the accessibility aids are already in place before a person needs them, their presence will be one less stressor to process when the time of need comes.

We hear of even healthy people slipping and falling in the bathtub, resulting in an injury. What if we had standard grab bars in bathtubs, preventing some of those injuries? My good friend said they even themselves sometimes use the grab bar installed in their bathtub for a disabled family member. By making features such as grab bars more common in showers and bathtubs, we not only enhance the safety of the non-disabled, but we take away some of the fear of aging or disability by creating familiarity through exposure. Grab bars could be beneficial in bathtubs not only in the home but also in hotels and other rentals. Making grab bars standard in every hotel or vacation rental bathtub or shower would benefit the safety and liability of all parties, ages, and physical abilities.

Some groups advocate the benefits of accessibility features for all of society. In the public arena, when sloped curbs were introduced for wheelchairs, people suddenly discovered that bikes no longer had to straddle curbs, and parents with strollers could maneuver sidewalks more easily. More and more people continue to benefit from structures and technology that help people with disabilities.

Hector Minto, a senior technology evangelist for accessibility at Microsoft, has worked in the field of accessibility and assistive technology for twenty years. He believes inclusive design can benefit everyone. Hector says when designers design with someone with permanent disabilities in mind, they end up with something that benefits many. He himself uses Sticky Keys on his computer because they make certain Windows shortcuts easier to access. Sticky Keys also provide users the ability to capitalize with one hand by making the shift function "hold" so the user does not have to press the shift and a letter down at the same time. Hector points out that sticky keys can benefit someone who has injured their wrist as well as someone who is holding a cup of coffee in one hand.

Hector uses the dictation feature regularly, and he finds the Read Aloud feature comes in handy for multitasking or listening to documents to check for errors. He also uses the greyscale mode that cuts out distractions. In addition, Windows has focus settings that can set a timer or turn off notifications. These can come in handy for getting work done or reducing the stress of notifications. Hector points out that all of these features increase productivity for everyone.

I have used the Sticky Keys feature for several years. My fellow authors and I utilize the Read Aloud feature for an extra layer of proofreading because hearing the text can help identify errors the eyes missed.

As society becomes more inclusive, I'm excited about what that means for our future, with everyone interacting and benefiting from one another, whether age one or one hundred one, whether a gymnast or wheelchair user. Whitney Bailey, host of the podcast *Spastic Chatter*, who has cerebral palsy and is an advocate of disability awareness, shared that she recently went on a vacation at the beach with her family. She was surprised to find people coming up to her and holding conversations with her instead of talking about her to the people she was with. When she mentioned her surprise to her family, her fourteen-year-old nephew said society's views are shifting and becoming more inclusive.

To promote awareness and integration, the United Nations Decade of Healthy Ageing (2021-2030) has formed a global collaboration to improve the lives of older people, their families, and their communities. Leaders are on a mission to add life to the years of the aging all over the world. Through this platform, they are creating awareness and taking action to create age-friendly environments (friendly to all ages); to combat ageism (stereotyping, prejudice, and discrimination toward people on the basis of their age); to promote integrated care, which coordinates care between different health and social care providers; and to strengthen good-quality, long-term care. One of their goals is:

> To create age-friendly environments that allow older people to age safely in a place that is right for them, continue to develop personally, be included, and contribute to their communities while retaining their independence and health in a way that cultivates their optimum benefit.

Let's keep working on evolving into a more inclusive society. Doing things such as incorporating features in the home to benefit aging in place not only serves the occupants but could also help visiting friends and relatives, thus opening up opportunities for bonding relationships where society no longer has to miss out on the knowledge, wisdom, strengths, and community of one another due to mobility barriers. Recognizing the strengths of all people, no matter their age, ability, or disability, will allow us to foster a world of strength and vitality.

Discussion

1. Recall an embarrassing moment and how you felt inside. Write about that experience.

_____

_____

_____

_____

2. What coping strategies for embarrassment discussed in this chapter resonated as ones that would be helpful for you?

_____

_____

_____

_____

3. What could you say or do to help someone the next time you sense they are embarrassed?

_____

_____

_____

_____

4. If you have a disability or are living with a chronic illness, list at least three strengths your life challenge has cultivated within you.

_____

_____

_____

_____

5. Now, if you have a disability or are living with a chronic illness, ask two people what strengths they see in you.

They can be any strengths, not only ones cultivated by your challenge. Write down those strengths.

_____

_____

_____

_____

6. If you are not disabled and do not have a chronic illness, think of someone who faces those challenges and list the strengths you see in them.

_____

_____

_____

_____

7. If you are not disabled, what features in society to improve accessibility to the disabled have you found personally beneficial?

_____

_____

_____

_____

8. If you are not disabled, do you feel including grab bars and other accessibility features in the home in the absence of need is a good idea? Would you like to include any of these features in your home?

_____

_____

_____

_____

9. If you are disabled, are there any accessibility features you do not presently have in your home that would make your home a safer place or a place where you could move with more ease? If so, list the features needed or the problems you are encountering. If you listed features or problems, begin a conversation with your doctor, family, or friends about your needs.

_____

_____

_____

_____

Poems

Wrap Your Mind Around Love

Wrap your mind around love
While love wraps its mind around you.
Love says you are accepted.
Love says it is true.

Love heals wounds of anger.
Love drives out your fear.
Love heals all shame.
Love wipes away your tears.

Love holds you gently.
Love shows you what's true.
Wrap your mind around love
While love wraps its mind around you.

View a video of "Wrap Your Mind Around Love" at
https://youtu.be/ZciPH3Td49I?

We Rest Our Case

We are the world,
A people of one human race,
Differences in body, ability,
Beliefs, thoughts, and values.
But upon the unison of
Our need for love and peace,
We rest our case.

Calling Heaven to Earth

We call heaven to earth,
Peace be upon us now.
Unity in spirit,
Carnality, take a bow.

Bowing in surrender,
Surrendering to truth,
Truth that lies within us
Birthed within to soothe.

The truth of compassion,
The truth of joyful souls,
The truth of love in action,
This truth creates our goals.

This truth of gentle kindness,
This truth of a generous act,
This truth of full-out meekness,
This truth of patience's impact.

This goodness born within us
Calling heaven to earth.
Heaven, come, dwell among us
With priceless value and worth.

Chapter 9
Cultivating Connections

FTER COVID STARTED, SOME MEMES on social media depicted the reactions of introverts versus extroverts to the shutdown and social distancing. Introverts were pictured as ecstatic; extroverts were pictured as disheartened. These memes struck a chord as hilarious but so true of the human condition. I totally resonated with the introvert who was ecstatic.

I was in the early stages of my healing journey, and this opportunity for time away from the world to heal fit right into what I needed. I am grateful for what COVID-19 did to speed up the acceptance of virtual meetings, virtual socialization, and health care. This taught society the power of connecting even though not in person. Mental health care professionals were able to glean confirmation that virtual connections carry benefits and power. Gone are the notions that church attendance has to be in-person only, that every health care appointment needs physical presence, and that deep connections can only be felt in person. Physical presence does carry extra energy, but virtual meeting is a valuable option.

We saw the advent of virtually sharing meals together, the beauty of virtually worshipping together, and we even discovered the outright fun of hosting virtual birthday parties. We connected, we explored, and we learned.

In 2019, when I joined Talkspace, I got my feet wet and my mind acclimated to the idea of mental health services via the internet, a service that had been lurking in the background of society. My Talkspace relationship was through messaging; no video was the service plan I had chosen. Therefore, 2020 still brought the newness of video meetings to me.

In 2020, through encouragement from my Talkspace therapist and my primary care doctor, I established virtual care via video platform with a registered dietitian. When my Talkspace therapist ended her tenure with Talkspace, I chose to seek care from a psychologist through video meetings. My meetings with my psychologist were conducted through a platform designed and dedicated to medical care services.

In 2022, when my cousin Jaci Lamont shared on social media that she was writing a book and inviting people to meet with her in a Zoom group to give her feedback for her book, I was excited for her and interested in the opportunity, but I shied away from the idea at first because Zoom still seemed like a trepidatious endeavor. I thought things like, *If I press this button, will I lose connection and not be able to get back into the meeting? If I hit that button, will my computer shut down? How do I adjust the volume? Will I look stupid, like I don't know what I'm doing?* The comforting truth to the last question is a lot of us still don't know what we are doing with all of the virtual world's features and the new features being added frequently.

However, I had a strong pull to meet with Jaci's group, fueled by my love of books and my own interest in writing. Writing was a dream I had set aside because I thought it would not happen. I couldn't say no to the pull of joining my cousin's group, so at what I thought was the last minute, I asked her if I could join, fearing I was too late. I was not too late. And by reason of use, my senses became exercised to use Zoom more peacefully and skillfully.

After learning from Jaci about book coaching, I discovered an upcoming online book challenge being held by her coach. By then, inspired by Jaci's endeavors to write her book, I had in mind that it was possible I could write a book. I joined the book challenge and then joined the coaching program of the book publishing coach.

Accountability Group

As part of the book coaching program, we gain the opportunity to meet and develop relationships with all of the other authors in the program. We also have an accountability group, usually consisting of the people who joined the program at the same time. The group meets at hours and intervals best suited for its members. The group I am in consists of a strong cohesion of support, integration, and collaboration.

The skills and knowledge of our group members blend beautifully together. We offer advice and support to one another. And we dream together of possibilities, which is exciting. The heart's desire of each of our members is to bring a message of hope through their books and to share the knowledge of the powerful things they have learned in their lives.

Value of Connections

Connections are vital to the human experience. That is how we are designed. We need each other to thrive. We strengthen one another through support and inspiration. No one single person possesses all the knowledge needed to live their lives. Life requires learning new information as we encounter new experiences. Sharing our knowledge deepens growth. Receiving knowledge and support from others, whether it's to bolster our good experiences or to aid us in challenging situations, not only deepens our growth but deepens the growth of the giver. We are gifts to one another.

My life has been enriched by making deeper connections. Feeling seen and heard and having a sense of belonging brings joy. In the past, I had never known that I felt alone. I had done as prescribed by society and kept a degree of social activity, the degree chosen and afforded by my level of introversion and mental and emotional health, but I found I had not made the deep connections. We hear that people can feel alone in the midst of a group of people. I felt alone and didn't know it. This was due to trauma.

We can be unaware of traumas and wounds in our subconscious minds blocking our ability to connect. Those same wounds can also prevent us from finding the people we can deeply connect with because we are not seeking or allowing ourselves to find those connections. We may also find those deep connections but not hold onto them by pushing them away instead of inviting them in to remain and grow. But we can heal, we can learn, and we can receive revelation and wisdom to make connections and to let connections happen.

I realized the depth and power of aloneness one morning after I had met with my authors' accountability group. I'm still growing in voice and how to release and share the thoughts in my head. As the conversation proceeded, I would resonate with things and recall information I had learned that would fit right in. However, I listened to the old message that said it was too much effort to put my thoughts into words and get the message out, or try to step into the discussion, so I will just sit here and enjoy the conversation. Our group shares a cohesion that joyfully welcomes and values every thought anyone shares, so my hesitation was just totally me not making an effort to share.

After we ended our Zoom call, I went about doing some housework and realized I felt an emptiness, a sadness, and a loss of appetite. As I reflected, I realized how familiar the feeling was, and how it always seemed to occur after times of human interaction with a missed opportunity to form connection. Then I realized the feeling was a feeling of loneliness brought on by neglecting to connect. I learned, in that moment, yet another lesson about the importance of connection and how beautiful it is to cherish connections and engage in moments of connection whenever we have the opportunity.

The cornerstone of good mental health is quality connections with yourself and others. We need to develop close connections with people who both see and hear us. That was one of the first things I learned in counseling. People need to be both seen and heard. It is a fundamental human need that has been widely studied in the field of psychology. Being seen and heard refers to the human desire to be acknowledged, recognized, and understood by others. Being seen and heard also ties in with the fundamental human need for connection. Connection fosters a sense of belonging, the feeling of being understood, and the joy of having close relationships.

When we feel unseen and unheard, it can lead to feeling lonely, socially isolated, and disconnected. These feelings can negatively affect mental health and well-being because social connections are essential for emotional regulation, stress management, and overall psychological health.

As I've reflected on connecting, I see the beauty of the way connections calm the mind and smooth out the plains of emotional regulation. At times when I've been in a stressful situation or something made me nervous, just a smile, laugh, or hello from someone has broken that stress and helped calm me. The more extensive the connection, such as a deep conversation, the greater the benefit will be. In order for connections to calm the mind, we have to allow them to do so. If we reject the opportunity to calm our minds and choose instead to continue carrying our stress, we will bear the consequences of mental anxiety and its repercussions on our physical bodies. People with strong social connections are more resilient to stress, have better emotional regulation, and are less likely to experience mental health problems such as depression and anxiety.

Levels of Connectedness

Scientists have proposed three levels of social connectedness: intimate connectedness, relational connectedness, and collective connectedness. To this list I will add global connectedness. As we review these four levels, perhaps you can think of people and groups in your life who fit into these categories.

1. **Intimate connectedness:** This is the perceived closeness to a nurturing companion who affirms our value as an individual. These people can include a spouse, companion, or anyone with whom you share a deep mutual bond of affection and trust. We will generally spend 40 percent of our time with five of our intimate connections.

2. **Relational connectedness:** This is a perceived sense of friends or family members who provide mutual aid and support. These relationships are more casual but still provide closeness and can be relied upon for substantial support such as childcare, car breakdowns, and do-it-yourself-building

projects. These relationships typically number fifteen to fifty people.

3. **Collective collectedness:** This is the perceived presence of a meaningful connection with a group of people. These groups can include such conglomerations as teams, volunteer groups, schools, places of worship, and online support groups. Interacting with a community of people who share common interests or goals contributes to our collective identity and makes us feel part of something larger than ourselves. Research shows the more groups we voluntarily belong to, the more likely we are to report a higher level of social connectedness. This third level of connectedness generally consists of 150-1500 people.

4. **Global connectedness:** We share connectedness with every human being. We all consist of the same materials of blood, skin, muscles, brain, and organs. We all have a mind, and we all have a spirit. Those factors unite us. And we all bring a unique presence into the world.

We can best discover our own unique presence in our place of peace. Great power within and without is found in the presence of peace. A lifetime is not long enough to fully bring a message of peace to the entire planet, but with our efforts to bring peace within our own selves and share the message of peace with those whom we can, we can continue uniting with our Creator in the present time to promote the creation of peace on earth until time with no end.

Seek Balance

In life, we will live best by seeking balance in all things. Avoid extremes, avoid judging others, and avoid allowing others' judgments to deter you from your balance. Filter all judgments to discern if they are good and true. Receive wisdom from others and from your Maker or Source. Continue to ask, seek, and knock for the things you don't know. Look within to find your peace and to meet with your Creator. Keep digging into that secret place inside where he dwells in communion with you. Keep reaching deep within and bringing out your abundance; keep bringing out your treasures and gold and hide them no more. We need you. The world needs the whole, the healed you, and you need you too. That you is the you who fulfills you through your uncovered joys and your unburied treasures.

"Reaching deep within you, bringing out the gold;
you are not too young now, and you are not too old…"

— Tracy Rohrer Irons, "The Shadow of Time"

Discussion

1. Name people in your intimate and relational connectedness levels.

_____

_____

_____

_____

2. Name people in your collective connectedness level.

_____

_____

_____

_____

3. Share any thoughts or opinions you have about global connectedness.

_____

_____

_____

_____

Poem

Who's Runnin' 'Round?

The enemy, he stole from me.
He took away what's mine.
He told me I would miss it none.
He told me I'd be fine.

He took away my confidence.
He took away my worth.
He hid away some golden gifts,
And even took some mirth.

He gave to me confusion,
To keep me runnin' 'round.
Then he slipped out my back door
And, lastly, clean left town.

Time did pass day by day.
It rained; it poured some more.
Then I decided I'd had enough,
And I walked out my back door.

I gathered all my strength,
And then I, too, left town.
I pulled up my bootstraps
And went to hunt him down.

I found right where he did reside.
I walked into his camp.
I demanded back the spoils he took.
I found them with my lamp.

My land it was restored to me,
The potholes all filled in.
Now I've got the victory.
I declare I win!

Chapter 10
Anticipating the Future

"Life is a dance; come and dance with me."
— Zana Kenjar

T HIS LAST CHAPTER HAS TURNED into a bit of a coffee talk chapter, so feel free to pour yourself a cup of coffee and join me right back here.

In concluding this book, I want to emphasize the importance of seeking out your own path on your journey to you. I have shared tools and ideas that helped me, but you are you, so what works best for you may be different tools or variations of the ones that worked for me. The vast expanse of the world at our fingertips today excites me. Use that opportunity to continue to explore and grow your own healing and daily practices that keep you connected to you because knowing you is your most important task in life. Knowing you is where your truest love, joy, peace, inspiration, gifts, and talents come from. In knowing yourself, you can fuel that river of living water that flows out of you, giving life to both yourself and others.

I posed the thought earlier that when we set out on our journey to heal an eating disorder, we want to know how it started. An eating disorder functions as an addiction, so we can say the same for other addictions. As I revealed earlier, a complex web of factors plays into an eating disorder.

The best explanation I have for how my eating disorder started became clear to me in reverse order. After I healed my relationship with food and food became a friend—a friend that nourishes this body I love because it houses my mind and the joys, aspirations, gifts, and abilities that lie within it and my spirit—I realized my focus and attention turn to other activities and events throughout my day and my hunger cues get pushed aside and ignored unless I consciously try to stay aware of them.

It is normal and healthy for our attention to be on other things so we are only reminded of food when our bodies start signaling hunger. My curiosity draws my attention to other thoughts and tasks, and the extra energy and focus it takes for my brain to make my body move, due to disability, all draw my attention away from my body's call for food; then I sometimes continue with my task in my drive to get it done and not notice my hunger. I have now set a reminder alarm for noon each day to remind me to focus, as needed, on my hunger cues.

When I was thirteen, I was thriving with my own interests and school, and probably facing some of the emotional struggles a typical thirteen-year-old faces as they enter the teen years. As a deformity with my foot set in and progressed, my attention to hunger cues was diverted to attending to my struggles. Because I was not talking about my struggles but burying them, and because I, like many, was caught in the environment of society's diet culture, my mind latched onto the distraction of food and body image that gave me relief from facing my personal physical and emotional struggles.

Some people engage in self-harm as a coping mechanism; my method of self-harm became starving myself because pushing through hunger pangs and past blood sugar lows helped relieve my mental struggles.

Then, untreated, it all became a mixed-up, tangled pattern where food became an enemy and body image and weight became an obsession. As the years progressed, I continued to be locked out of full access to the real me housed in my peace, joy, and truths because I continued to engage with the coping mechanism that kept me in the lies of what I thought I was supposed to be—a person with a thriving career, able body, and abundant social engagements. My grief and disappointment at not achieving what I thought I was supposed to drove me further away from attaining the beautiful things life had in store for me. Their beauty was wrapped in a different package than the one I was looking for. I finally surrendered in healing and sat down to open the package, and now I can rise up more and more in who I am. In healing, we grow and relearn to love ourselves, and hold dear, in appreciation, the life-giving value of who we are. I can now continuously access and grow self-worth, self-confidence, and inner passions instead of obtaining only intermittent access, as before.

In this new space of life, I'm now freer to explore who I really am. Hiding within an eating disorder, or any addiction or distraction, robs us of our real selves. The addiction can even be something like workaholism; some may term it as a more glorious addiction, but really it is not. All addictions and anything that pulls us away from our true selves and from attending to the real, lovely, deep, hard, joyous, wise, sincere, complex, gut-wrenching, and strengthening truths of life rob us of our deepest selves.

After living with the heartache of diminished joy and tainted peace in the absence of access to my deepest being,

I am passionate about reaching in and discovering your truest self and living from the core of who you are—living from the goodness of you. Let's heal the wounds, heal the hurts, heal the trauma, heal the grief, and anger. We can pave the land inside of us with love, joy, peace, compassion, patience, gentleness, and goodness. A good list for interior resources I find helpful is the Fruit of the Spirit in Galatians 5:22-23: love, joy, peace, patience, kindness, goodness, faith, gentle humility and respect, and temperance/moderation with balance.

We can befriend and respect anger, grief, and sadness by learning to heed their messages. These messengers were sent to help us tend to the needs they point out. Being in touch with your deepest you is a lifelong journey. It's an ongoing discovery.

I still work with a mental health therapist as I more clearly and openly navigate through my disability. I also talk with her about the discoveries that hung me up before. Recently, I discovered avoidant attachment style is the name of the psychological pattern I've experienced and described in this book. Naming it sheds even more light on it for me.

A few months ago, I came across an interview Sarah Cavanaugh of Peaceful Exit conducted with Dr. Jill Bolte Taylor on the subject of "Your Brain and Death." I'm eager to listen to any interviews with Dr. Jill Bolte Taylor, so I tuned in. The interview was excellent, so I decided to share it with my therapist since the Peaceful Exit platform deals with death and, inadvertently, grief. My therapist not only specializes in eating disorders but has a special interest in grief. She mentioned that maybe I should explore the Peaceful Exit podcast and materials more because exploration of grief could be beneficial. I put the thought in my head to chew on while I finished my book with the intention of *maybe after I finish my book.*

During solar eclipse week, I engaged in a virtual yoga and meditation practice. The practice started with yoga before venturing into meditation. As we rested down into our bodies and began moving, I felt a wave of grief come over me as a familiar longing came to mind, a craving to move my body freely and fluidly. Then I thought, *There it is, right there it is.* And it felt like a key of revelation. Bessel van der Kolk's landmark work on trauma crossed my mind, particularly his discovery that yoga can help trauma heal. In *The Body Keeps the Score*, Van der Kolk shares that yoga has the power, through its movements and methods, to allow a person to reconnect with their body, where trauma is stored, and to heal trauma and grief.

A few days after that yoga practice, I heard a discussion that inspired me. I've shared earlier that I am a person who does not look back, but I look at where I am now and how I go forward. We know the wisdom in going forward from where we are now because we cannot change the past. Coupled with my intention of dealing with the now and going forward was a fear that if I looked at the *what-ifs* of the past, I might get stuck in them. In the discussion I heard, I was struck by the courage, wisdom, and therapeutic effect that could be wrought by looking at the possibilities of *what if this were different or that was different?* So, I chose a few spots in life and experimented. I found this exercise brought healing and relief instead of grief. It reminded me again that life is spacious, and it allowed me to feel less stuck in the details. One aspect of life I experimented with was, *What if I were not disabled?* The first thought that came to mind was maybe I would have been in ballet or been a runner. I reflected back again to that smooth, fluid, beautiful movement of ballet or that freedom of running, body in motion, and wind against your face. My sisters were in track in school, and I briefly thought, even back then, that maybe I would have been in track. I forgot about that until now. A brief foray into *what if*, and that is all I am doing for now because I'm doing me in this journey of life.

A friend and I recently discussed that everything in life has both gains and losses. While we can consider the possible losses of a challenging circumstance, we can also consider the gains that resulted from its occurrence. Since I was a child, my heart has been touched by the kindness and compassion of others, from people who hold doors open at stores and other locations to the ones who offer to help put groceries in the car. I wrote earlier of the compassion of the one who helped me up at school when I fell down. Then there are the doctors who give an extra special touch to their patients' care.

I have author friends literally from coast to coast. Last year, I had the incredible privilege of meeting one of my author friends in person here in Indiana where she was speaking at a women's retreat. We roomed together at the retreat along with one of her friends (now my friend). I was so touched by the purity of their compassion. In their kind, sincere, and gentle way, they both often asked me, "Can we do anything for you?" Both of them have studied brain science as part of their professions, so they are aware of the conscious and subconscious challenges a new environment can create for the brain-body connection. Above that, they are simply both wonderful, caring people. And their thoughtful, caring ways touched my heart.

I'm thankful for the ways the warmheartedness of others inspires us in our everyday lives and carries us through our storms. The other day, I was in the middle of the day going about my tasks and lightly thinking of a matter I'm trying to sort out in my mind. As I proceeded to turn around, all of a sudden, from that place of the still small voice inside of each one of us, I heard, "The storm's not over, yet." That stopped me in my tracks. I knew it was a message about the subject in my mind, and what struck me even more was the clarity that came from recognizing and naming it as a storm. Not only does that give my mind an extra grip on processing it, but it allowed me to see *storm* in a new definition. I previously viewed storms in our lives as waves-thrashing, man-almost-overboard tempests. But this helped me to understand that even when we are processing our questions or uncertainties in a more peaceful state, they are still storms.

Many, if not all, of our storms in life include an element of grief. As I am trying to close this book, thoughts keep coming to my mind and I think, "Oh, that would be good to share in the book." Early on, our book coach told us that a book has the potential of never being done. You can be adding, editing, and polishing a book forever. But it comes to the point where you just have to call it done. Yesterday, while thinking about the *storm* definition, I thought, "Oh, I could write another chapter and call it *Grieving: Your Way Through the Storm.*" (And my mind swelled up into a wow face emoji.) But a few hours later, I told myself, "Tracy, you do not need to write another chapter; you need to finish the book." This book is a snapshot in time. Before long, I may have new growth, new discoveries, and new revelations as I continue to build upon life, like we all do.

I'm happy to report I recently got a van equipped in a fashion that allows me to get my walker in and out of my van myself. I'll be on the road again, and my goal is to go to the gym and maybe physical therapy. Beyond that, my author friends and I have goals and aspirations and are always coming up with some wild and crazy ideas to make our dreams happen. As Bessel van der Kolk says, "Imagination gives us the opportunity to envision new possibilities—it is an essential launchpad for making our hopes come true."

I love the story Jamie Kern Lima shares in her new book, *Worthy* (print and Audible copies released February 2024), of how a caterpillar becomes a butterfly. The caterpillar creates a cocoon, and inside the cocoon, it secretes enzymes and liquifies itself. Then, its body is rebuilt as it is transformed into a butterfly. Upon exiting the cocoon, the butterfly's wings are wet, and it remains very vulnerable to prey until its wings dry and it can fly. As I listened to the book on Audible, I said to myself, "Hey, wait; I wrote a poem about a butterfly!" So, I looked up the poem, and I'd like to share it with you to help you fly too. I wrote this on July 28, 2023:

Butterfly

I am just a butterfly;
I broke out of a shell.
I once was a caterpillar,
Which I thought was swell.

But my God had other plans—
Dreams of what I could be.
So he crafted, and he formed me,
Then he set me free.

He gave me wings to fly
To new heights way up high,
To share beauty
In no tour of duty,

But in joyous delight,
Together with God's might,
To push back the night
And bring forth the light.

In unison with creation,
Let us engage in the curation
Of the bonding beauty
Of authenticity.

Spread your wings and fly!

Life is a wonderful journey, and this book shares only a speck of all of the tools and resources life has to offer us in our pursuit of being the true self each one of us was birthed to be. You are here by design to share the voice of who you are: the love, compassion, passions, joy, creativity, knowledge, and all of the beauty of who you are. We are so excited you are here!

Poem

Thank You, Morning Sunshine

Thank you, morning sunshine,
Thank you from my heart.
You shared your thoughts within you,
Your wisdom to impart.

With radiance of hope and wonder,
You inspired my heart.
You shared your true essence.
You shared it from the start.

I listen each morning to you,
You fill me from within.
That still, small voice within me,
It speaks and calls again.

We walk beside still waters,
We lie in pastures green,
We climb the tallest mountains,
And view the wonders seen.

The vista lies within me,
Its beauties I behold.
I wrap my arms around it,
Its treasures make me bold.

I know you emit God's glory,
And these gifts were made by God.
I have full access to
This clay, this wondrous sod.

References

Chapter 1

"Benefit Planned for Rohrer Girl." *Elkhart Truth* (Elkhart, IN). November 23, 1976.

"Benefit for Tracy Rohrer." *Nappanee Advance-News* (Nappanee, IN). November 18, 1976: 4.

Chapter 2

Uttekar, Pallavi Suyog, MD. "What Is Classified as an Eating Disorder?" MedicineNet. https://www.medicinenet.com/what_is_classified_as_an_eating_disorder/article.htm. Accessed March 26, 2024.

Farrow, Claire V., Jennifer Yee, and Suman Das. "Cultural Influences on Body Dissatisfaction and Eating Disorders: A Review." *Eating Disorders*. 25.5 (2017): 395-412.

Gutierrez-Maldonado, José, Luis Villaseñor-Pineda, and Gabriela L. Rodríguez-González. "Genetic and Environmental Factors in the Etiology of Eating Disorders." *Frontiers in Psychiatry*. 8 (2017): 411.

Lopez, Teresa A., Natalia Guzman, and Maria Smith. "Risk and Protective Factors for Eating Disorders: A Meta-Analysis." *Clinical Psychology Review*. 45 (2016): 1-12.

Gross, Richard S. and Paul D. Hastings. "The Role of Life Events in the Onset and Maintenance of Eating Disorders." *Clinical Psychology Review*. 25.2 (2005): 141-169.

Lock, James, Daniel Le Grange, W. Stewart Agras, and Christopher Dare. "Psychological Predictors of Treatment Outcome in Adolescents with Anorexia Nervosa." *Journal of Consulting and Clinical Psychology*. 69.3 (2001): 479-487.

Cross River Therapy. "Eating Disorder Statistics." https://www.crossrivertherapy.com/eating-disorder-statistics. Accessed February 7, 2024.

Holland, Kimberly. "Is Anorexia Genetic?" Healthline. Last modified June 24, 2022. https://www.healthline.com/health/eating-disorders/is-anorexia-genetic. Accessed May 25, 2024.

National Association of Anorexia Nervosa and Associated Disorders. "Eating Disorder Statistics." https://anad.org/eating-disorder-statistic/. Accessed February 7, 2024.

PeaceHealth. "Immunizations." https://www.peacehealth.org/medical-topics/id/immun. Accessed February 7, 2024.

Tribole, E. and E. Resch. *Intuitive Eating: A Revolutionary Program That Works*. 3rd ed. New York: St. Martin's Griffin, 2012.

Change, Chia-Yu, Der-Shin Ke, and Jen-Yin Chen. "Essential Fatty Acids and Human Brain." *Acta Neurol Taiwan*. 18. 4 (2009): 231-241. https://pubmed.ncbi.nlm.nih.gov/20329590/#. Accessed February 7, 2024.

Linus Pauling Institute. "Macronutrient Information Center." Last modified April 1, 2020. https://lpi.oregonstate.edu/mic/health-disease/cholesterol#. Accessed February 7, 2024.

Moriarty, Colleen. "Vitamin D Myths 'D'-bunked." Yale Medicine. March 15, 2018. https://www.yalemedicine.

org/news/vitamin-d-myths-debunked. Accessed February 7, 2024.

American College of Cardiology and American Heart Association. "2019 ACC/AHA Guideline on the Primary Prevention of Cardiovascular Disease: Executive Summary." Last modified November 11, 2019. https://www.acc.org/latest-in-cardiology/articles/2019/11/11/19/24/2019-accaha-guideline-on-the-primary-prevention-of-cardiovascular-disease-executive-summary. Accessed February 7, 2024.

Mayo Clinic. "LDL Cholesterol: 'Bad' Cholesterol." Last modified October 13, 2020. https://www.mayoclinic.org/diseases-conditions/high-blood-cholesterol/in-depth/ldl-cholesterol/ART-20046388. Accessed February 7, 2024.

Mayo Clinic. "HDL Cholesterol: 'Good' Cholesterol." Last modified October 13, 2020. https://www.mayoclinic.org/diseases-conditions/high-blood-cholesterol/in-depth/hdl-cholesterol/ART-20055770. Accessed February 7, 2024.

Chapter 3

Christian Standard Bible. Bible Gateway. BibleGateway.com. Accessed February 14, 2024.

van der Kolk, Bessel. *The Body Keeps the Score: Brain, Mind, and Body in the Healing of Trauma.* New York: Viking Press, 2014.

"Drama." Merriam-Webster. https://www.merriam-webster.com/dictionary/drama. Accessed February 14, 2024.

Center for Health Care Strategies. "What Is Trauma?" Trauma-Informed Care Implementation Resource Center. https://www.traumainformedcare.chcs.org/. Accessed February 14, 2024.

Watson, Kathryn. "Abandonment Trauma: Effects and Symptoms in Children and Adults." *Psych Central.*

May 24, 2022. https://psychcentral.com/health/abandonment-trauma. Accessed February 14, 2024.

Lenora, K. M. March 7, 2022. "What Are Abandonment Issues? Causes, Symptoms, and How to Overcome." https://thriveworks.com/blog/abandonment-issues/. Accessed February 14, 2024.

Nationwide Children's Hospital. "Family Resources & Education." https://www.nationwidechildrens.org/family-resources/support-programs. Accessed February 14, 2024.

Mulder, P. (2018). "Wheel of Emotions by Robert Plutchik Explained: Theory, Example." Toolshero. Retrieved [3/17/2023] from https://www.toolshero.com/psychology/wheel-of-emotions-plutchik/. Accessed February 14, 2024.

Karimova, Hokuma. "The Emotion Wheel: What It Is and How to Use It." *Positive Psychology*. December 24, 2017. https://positivepsychology.com/emotion-wheel/#test-wheel-of-emotions. Accessed February 14, 2024.

ManageTrainLearn. "What Your Emotions Are Sent to Teach You." https://www.managetrainlearn.com/masterclass/view/what-your-emotions-are-sent-to-teach-you/. Accessed February 14, 2024.

Bergland, Christopher. "The 90-Second Rule Builds Self-Control." *Psychology Today*. April 9, 2020. https://www.psychologytoday.com/ca/blog/the-right-mindset/202004/the-90-second-rule-builds-self-control. Accessed February 14, 2024.

Manson, Mark. "Understanding Your Emotions." Mark Manson. https://markmanson.net/understanding-your-emotions. Accessed February 14, 2024.

Workplace Strategies for Mental Health. "The Functions of Emotions." https://www.workplacestrategiesformentalhealth.com/resources/the-functions-of-emotions. Accessed February 14, 2024.

Psych Central. "Lessons Our Emotions Can Teach Us and How We Can Learn." https://psychcentral.com/blog/lessons-our-emotions-can-teach-us-and-how-we-can-learn#1. Accessed February 14, 2024.

van der Kolk, Bessel, MD. "Definition of Trauma." Mountain Creative Arts Counseling. https://www.mountaincreativearts.com/definition-of-trauma/#. Accessed February 14, 2024.

Mountain Creative Arts Counseling. "Effects of Trauma." https://www.mountaincreativearts.com/effects-of-trauma/. Accessed February 14, 2024.

Chapter 4

WebMD. "What to Know About OCD in Children." https://www.webmd.com/children/what-to-know-about-ocd-in-children. Accessed February 18, 2024.

American Psychiatric Association. *Diagnostic and Statistical Manual of Mental Disorders, 5th ed*. Arlington, VA: American Psychiatric Publishing, 2013.

Abramowitz, Jonathan S., Steven Taylor, and Dean McKay. "Obsessive-Compulsive Disorder." *The Lancet*. 374.9688 (2009): 491-499.

Franklin, Martin E., Edna B. Foa, and John S. March. "The Pediatric Obsessive-Compulsive Disorder Treatment Study: Rationale, Design, and Methods." *Journal of Child and Adolescent Psychopharmacology*. 21.2 (2011): 111.

Koran, Lorrin M. et al. "Practice Guideline for the Treatment of Patients with Obsessive-Compulsive Disorder." *The American Journal of Psychiatry*. 164.7 Suppl (2007): 5.

Hertenstein, Elisabeth, Nicola Rose, and Ulrich Voderholzer. "Mindfulness-Based Cognitive Therapy in Obsessive-Compulsive Disorder—A Qualitative Study on Patients' Experiences." *BMC Psychiatry* 12 (2012): 185.

Klinger, Evelyne et al. "Virtual Reality Therapy Versus Cognitive Behavior Therapy for Social Phobia: A Preliminary Controlled Study." *CyberPsychology & Behavior*. 8.1 (2005): 77.

Chödrön, Pema. *When Things Fall Apart: Heart Advice for Difficult Times*. Narrated by Cassandra Campbell. New York, NY: Random House Audio, 2017.

Tafarodi, R. W. and W. B. Swann, Jr. "Two-Dimensional Self-Esteem: Theory and Measurement." *Personality and Social Psychology Review*. 5.2 (2001): 126-138.

Chapter 5

New International Version. Bible Gateway. BibleGateway.com. Accessed February 21, 2024.

Benarroch, Eduardo E. "The Vagus Nerve: Functional Organization and Involvement in Neurologic Disease." *Neurology*. 90.20 (2018): 948-959. doi: 10.1212/WNL.0000000000005606. Accessed February 21, 2024.

Tracey, Kevin J. "Physiology and Immunology of the Cholinergic Antiinflammatory Pathway." *Journal of Clinical Investigation*. 129.9 (2019): 3612-3620. doi: 10.1172/JCI130415. Accessed February 21, 2024.

Pajer, Nicole. "Mindfulness Quotes to Help You Reset and Reflect." *Parade*. parade.com/mindfulness-quotes. Accessed May 30, 2024.

Mason, A. E. et al. "Reduced Reward-Driven Eating Accounts for the Impact of a Mindfulness-Based Diet and Exercise Intervention on Weight Loss: Data from the SHINE Randomized Controlled Trial." *Appetite*. 100 (2016): 86-93. doi: 10.1016/j.appet.2016.02.009. Accessed February 21, 2024.

Kiecolt-Glaser, J. K. and R. Glaser. "Mindfulness-Based Stress Reduction for Healthy Individuals: What Do We Really Know?" *Brain, Behavior, and Immunity*. 24.6 (2010): 1044-1048. doi: 10.1016/j.bbi.2010.04.006. Accessed February 21, 2024.

Desmond, Adam. "A Hebrew Mindset." *Adam Desmond.* https://adamdesmond.wordpress.com/2016/05/07/a-hebrew-mindset/. Accessed February 21, 2024.

Taylor, Jill Bolte. *My Stroke of Insight.* New York, NY: New American Library, 2009.

Taylor, Jill Bolte. *Whole Brain Living: The Anatomy of Choice and the Four Characters That Drive Our Life.* Carlsbad, CA: Hay House, 2021.

Spangler, Ann and Lois Tverberg. *Sitting at the Feet of Rabbi Jesus: How the Jewishness of Jesus Can Transform Your Faith.* Grand Rapids, MI: Zondervan, 2009.

Pema. *When Things Fall Apart: Heart Advice for Difficult Times.* Narrated by Cassandra Campbell. New York, NY: Random House Audio, 2017.

Chapter 6

Physiopedia. "Trendelenburg Gait." https://www.physio-pedia.com/Trendelenburg_Gait. Accessed February 23, 2024.

Chapter 7

Forbes Health. "Best Wheelchair Lifts: Reviews and Cost." https://www.forbes.com/health/medical-supplies/best-wheelchair-lifts-for-vehicles/. Accessed February 25, 2024.

ConsumerAffairs. "Wheelchair Vans: Reviews and Costs." https://www.consumeraffairs.com/automotive/wheelchair-vans/. Accessed February 25, 2024.

American Academy of Ophthalmology. "What Is Nystagmus?" https://www.aao.org/eye-health/diseases/what-is-nystagmus. Accessed February 25, 2024.

Sankara Nethralaya. "Short Review on Optical Coherence Tomography." https://www.sankaranethralaya.org/insight/PDF%20Files/oct2015/Short%20Review%203.pdf. Accessed February 25, 2024.

Chapter 8

DiveThru. "Feeling Embarrassed: A Guide to Your Emotions." https://divethru.com/feeling-embarrassed-a-guide-to-your-emotions/. Accessed February 28, 2024.

"Embarrassed." Merriam-Webster. https://www.merriam-webster.com/dictionary/embarrassed. Accessed February 28, 2024.

"Embarrassment." *Psychology Today*. https://www.psychologytoday.com/ca/basics/embarrassment. Accessed February 28, 2024.

"Embarrassment: The Emotional Experience of Self-Consciousness." *Journal of Personality and Social Psychology*. 109.5 (2015): 707-727. doi: 10.1037/pspp0000040. Accessed February 28, 2024.

Soulières, I. et al. "The Level and Nature of Autistic Intelligence." *Psychological Science*. 22.1 (2011): 132-138. doi: 10.1177/0956797610395391. Accessed February 28, 2024.

"Autism Strengths: The Benefits of Being Autistic." They Are the Future. https://www.theyarethefuture.co.uk/autism-strengths/. Accessed February 28, 2024.

"Accessibility Spotlight: Hector Minto." Disability:IN. https://disabilityin.org/releases/accessibility-spotlight-hector-minto/. Accessed February 28, 2024.

Bailey, Whitney. "Happy Disability Pride Month!" YouTube Video, 2:59. Posted July 4, 2023. https://youtu.be/lakhIED_hSA?feature=shared. Accessed February 28, 2024.

"What Is the Decade?" Decade of Healthy Ageing. https://www.decadeofhealthyageing.org/about/about-us/what-is-the-decade. Accessed January 17, 2024.

Chapter 9

Baumeister, R. F. & M. R. Leary. "The Need to Belong: Desire for Interpersonal Attachments as a Fundamental Human Motivation." *Psychological Bulletin*. 117.3 (1995): 497-529.

Cacioppo, J. T. & W. Patrick. *Loneliness: Human Nature and the Need for Social Connection*. New York: W. W. Norton & Company, 2008. p. 123.

Holt-Lunstad, J., T. B. Smith, and J. B. Layton. (2010). "Social Relationships and Mortality Risk: A Meta-Analytic Review." *PLoS Medicine*. 7.7 (2010): e1000316.

Perry, Rose. "Social Connectedness 101: The Many Pathways to Social Connection." *The Creature Times*. March 18, 2021.

Chapter 10

Kenjar, Zana. *Becoming a Legacy Leader: A 10-Step Manager's Guide to Unlocking Limitless Opportunities*. Lake Placid, NY: Aviva Publishing, 2023.

Bolte Taylor, Jill. "Your Brain and Death with Dr. Jill Bolte Taylor." Peaceful Exit. https://www.peacefulexit.net/post/your-brain-and-death-with-dr-jill-bolte-taylor. Accessed April 18, 2024.

van der Kolk, Bessel. *The Body Keeps the Score: Brain, Mind, and Body in the Healing of Trauma*. New York: Viking Press, 2014.

Kern Lima, Jamie. *Worthy*. 2023. Narrated by Jamie Kern Lima. Audible.

"Caterpillar to Butterfly: Metamorphosis Explainer." *Scientific American*. https://www.scientificamerican.com/article/caterpillar-butterfly-metamorphosis-explainer/. Accessed April 18, 2024.

Resources for Mental Health and Eating Disorder Support

Suicide

If you or a loved one ever need immediate help for suicidal thoughts or are having a mental health crisis, in the United States, please call:

988 Suicide and Crisis Lifeline 988lifeline.org

They are available by phone, chat, and text 24/7.

Outside of the United States, please search for your country's crisis and suicide hotline.

Mental Health

Psychology Today Find a Provider

https://www.psychologytoday.com/us/therapists

Psychology Today hosts a large database of providers for all mental health needs. Users can search by condition and other criteria of preference. Not only can you find providers specializing in eating disorders, but you can find specialists for your other mental health needs as well.

Eating Disorders

National Eating Disorders Association (NEDA)

https://www.nationaleatingdisorders.org/

NEDA is a leading eating disorders organization and works to promote research, community building, and awareness. Their website contains a large amount of information and resources for individuals, loved ones, children, students, and educators. You will find an ample list of provider and referral resources to aid you in finding both mental health providers and dietitians throughout the United States specializing in eating disorders. One of the sites listed in their directory can even connect you with providers worldwide. NEDA has volunteer opportunities and also sponsors awareness and fundraising campaigns.

Registered Dietitian

I'm happy to share with you the dietitian who helped me. I'm grateful for her approach in leading people to love their bodies and appreciate food. As always, in your exploration, I encourage you to find providers who are the best fit for you.

Melissa Freer-Smith, RDN, LDN, ACE-CPT

Registered Dietitian Licensed in Illinois, Indiana, and Michigan

Certified Personal Trainer with American Council on Exercise

Available for in person and virtual sessions

Melissa has used a Health at Every Size approach to nutrition and movement therapy for eating disorder recovery since 2009. She also works with people who are interested in healing their relationship with food and their bodies with the understanding that we are all negatively impacted by diet culture.

Email mfreersmith@gmail.com

Trauma

I spoke of my cousin Jaci Lamont in Chapter 9. I'd like to give her honorary mention here as a therapist who counsels people who have experienced trauma.

Jaci Lamont is an LCSW, founder of Accelerated Healing, LLC, and is licensed in Indiana. She currently sees clients both in person and virtually and specializes in trauma/PTSD, parenting, and ADHD. At the time of this book's publication, Jaci can be found at growtherapy.com/provider/lstfx6kz9vqn/jaci-lamont. Jaci may navigate to additional platforms in the future. You can also reach her at her book's website www.HealYourHeartHealYourChild.com.

About the Author

TRACY ROHRER IRONS IS A writer, a poet, and the founder of Our Voices Creations LLC. She values the power of community, the joy in collaboration, and the importance of sharing the authenticity of who you are. She enjoys crafting words into works of depth that speak to hearts and pull out sparkling wires of inspiration. She can also often be found creating videos and visual designs.

Tracy has been hosting community poems sponsored by Our Voices Creations LLC and invites you to join in the poems at the online Our Voices Creations Community on Facebook. Your voice enriches the world, and you are welcome at Our Voices Creations.

Tracy is available for podcasts and interviews, and you can contact her to inquire about other speaking engagements. You are invited to visit her websites regularly and subscribe to her mailing list for updates on future products.

Tracy lives in Indiana.

To contact Tracy, visit:

TracyRohrerIrons.com
Ourvoicescreations.com
tracyrohrerirons@hotmail.com

www.ingramcontent.com/pod-product-compliance
Lightning Source LLC
Chambersburg PA
CBHW060916120626
46553CB00001B/342